The Nation's
Favourite
Carols

The Nation's Favourite

Carols

Songs of Praise

ANDREW BARR

LION

A Lion Book
an imprint of
Lion Hudson plc
Mayfield House, 256 Banbury Road,
Oxford OX2 7DH, England
www.lionhudson.com
ISBN 0 7459 5180 5

First edition 2005
10 9 8 7 6 5 4 3 2 1 0

A catalogue record for this book is available
from the British Library

Typeset in 11/14 Modern880BT

Printed and bound in Singapore

Contents

Foreword 6

Prologue 10

Away in a manger 13

Christians, awake 16

God rest you merry, gentlemen (*English traditional carol*) 20

Good King Wenceslas 25

Hark! the herald-angels sing 29

In dulci jubilo 33

In the bleak mid-winter 36

It came upon the midnight clear 41

Joy to the world 46

Long time ago in Bethlehem (*Mary's boy child*) 49

O come, all ye faithful 52

O holy night 56

O little town of Bethlehem 60

On Christmas night all Christians sing (*Sussex carol*) 64

Once in royal David's city 67

See, amid the winter's snow 72

See him lying on a bed of straw (*Calypso carol*) 76

Silent night 80

The holly and the ivy 85

While shepherds watched 87

Epilogue 92

The Top Twenty 95

Foreword

The Nation's Favourite Carols tells the stories behind the twenty most popular Christmas carols chosen by *Songs of Praise* enthusiasts. This book is for everyone who loves to join in with the singing on *Songs of Praise*, either from the comfort of their own homes or by coming along to a 'Big Sing' whenever they can. Singers or not, all are dedicated viewers, and it is to them – and to you if you are one of them – that this book is dedicated.

The search for the nation's favourite carol began in the glittering surroundings of London's Royal Albert Hall. One Sunday evening in autumn, over 5,000 singers and musicians greeted the programme's presenters, Pam Rhodes and Aled Jones, with thunderous applause for the start of the *Songs of Praise* 'Christmas Big Sing'. The State Trumpeters of the Life Guards in their plumed helmets sounded a spectacular fanfare, and then all eyes turned to the conductor, Paul Leddington Wright. On each side of the organ, from behind a forest of Christmas trees, rose the men of the Royal Choral Society, immaculately bow-tied but wingless, to lead everyone in 'Hark! the herald-angels sing'. Hearing the roar of over a thousand enthusiastic voices I began to wonder whether I had discovered the 'nation's favourite' already, but the search would not begin properly until the programme had ended, the Hall had emptied and the *Songs of Praise* production team had helped gather up the first of what were to be thousands of voting papers. I staggered off into the London night, laden with carrier bags stuffed to the brim. The work had begun.

The first count was interesting, as it seemed that the choice of 'favourite' would be greatly influenced by a beautiful duet that had been sung that night by Aled Jones and the young New Zealand singer, Hayley Westenra. A few weeks later, hundreds more voting papers completed in Ely Cathedral produced a quite different result, again probably affected by what the congregation had most enjoyed singing

that night. By the time readers of *Songs of Praise* magazine and visitors to a special *Songs of Praise* website had added their votes, it became clear that our 'favourite' carols are chosen for all sorts of reasons.

Listeners to a rival radio station voted in their tens of thousands for 'O holy night' after enjoying Aled Jones's rendition of the carol. (Indeed, such is Aled's popularity that I cannot help wondering whether the theme song from *The Snowman* might not have come top if the celebrity treble-turned-tenor

could still sing it!) Meanwhile, after another poll organized in 2003 by BBC Radio Essex, a special carol service was held to announce the result, complete with gold envelopes such as those used for the Oscar awards, and 'Silent night' came top. 'Silent night' was also voted the viewers' all-time favourite in the Christmas 1988 *Songs of Praise* from Wells Cathedral. As soon as I began the search, people told me without hesitation that this carol would come top in 2005, even when it was not their personal favourite.

Fortunately, there are also people who ignore the fashion or mood of the day and remain faithful to a carol that has deepened their understanding of Christmas or helped them keep a personal memory alive, as many moving letters received from *Songs of Praise* viewers have shown. My neighbour Margaret has a memory about her favourite Christmas hymn, not because she heard it on *Songs of Praise* or in a broadcast from a famous university chapel, but because she enjoys her memories of singing it herself, along with her classmates, in a tiny schoolroom in the Scottish Borders. Her home was two miles away and she walked there and back every school day, even in the deepest, darkest days of winter, until the winter of 1947–48, when deep snowdrifts stopped classes. 'I liked singing "Once in royal David's city", and hearing the Christmas story again. Mrs Kidd, our teacher, played the piano, and if we took along a penny she would make a hot drink for us. It was lovely.'

This book is about the people who wrote the words and composed the music for our favourite carols, and about how, where and when these carols have captured our imagination. The universal message of Christmas touches us all in many different ways, and its effect is often best expressed in songs and music. As often as a Christmas carol unlocks an old memory, it is also true that familiar words and an old story have the power to affect us in new and profound ways in the light of the TV and radio headlines we wake up to each morning.

As always, my thanks to Morag Reeve, Nick Rous, Catherine Giddings and Rhoda Hardie at Lion Hudson, and to Hugh Faupel, Michael Wakelin and the *Songs of Praise* production team, who have joined me in this quest. Especial thanks to Liz, my wife, for whom this is a second book of popular carols, and to Kathleen Frew, whose skill in deciphering illegible notes written on buses and trains knows no limits. A final acknowledgment to my battered and bruised Olympus OM2 camera, which has survived the winter wild, and to Bernie Davies, BBC Lighting Director for *Songs of Praise*, who helped both it and me capture some of the magical atmosphere of the Christmas programmes.

As the popularity of carols waxes and wanes, this book takes them in alphabetical order; but their position in the top twenty of 2005 is included below each title.

I hope this little book on the background to the Christmas music you have chosen will remain a trusty guide in the years to come as you watch *Songs of Praise* and join in singing new and old favourite carols.

ANDREW BARR
Epiphany 2005

Prologue
A journey to the manger

Come, thou Redeemer of the earth,
And manifest thy virgin-birth:
Let every age adoring fall,
Such birth befits the God of all.

Nearing the end of a long journey south, I keep myself alert by singing all the words I can remember of an Advent hymn written by St Ambrose in the fourth century and translated by John Mason Neale – who also wrote the Christmas carol that I most enjoy singing. As the sun sets, I turn off the Great North Road from Edinburgh to London and head through the gathering gloom into the Fen country. Somewhere ahead is the *Songs of Praise* production team whom I hope to find camped out around the cathedral Church of the Holy and Undivided Trinity in Ely, where the citizens will soon be singing their Christmas carols.

So that I do not arrive late, I decide on a short cut that should take me in a straight line eastwards through the Fens to Ely. It is a bad plan. After a bewildering sequence of left and right turns, I realize I have lost all sense of direction. Not for the first time, I arrive at a railway level crossing with its gates firmly closed. Switching off the headlights while I wait for the train, I can now see thousands of stars in the huge sky. But which is the star in the East?

In Graham Swift's novel *Waterland*, set in the Fen country, the narrator begins by remembering an experience he had shared with his father in that flat, featureless region. They look up to where 'the sky swarmed with stars...' just like tonight, and he continues:

Dad said, 'Do you know what the stars are? They are the silver dust of God's blessing. They are broken-off bits of heaven. God cast them down to fall on us. But when he saw how wicked we were, he changed his mind and ordered the stars to stop. Which is why they hang in the sky, but seem as though at any time they might drop...'

The train flashes past, the gates open and I set off again under the huge display of 'broken-off bits of heaven'. During the next hour, as I zig-zag along roads that do not appear on my map with deep ditches full of water running on either side, I begin to think anything could happen in this mysterious landscape.

Since the seventh century Christians have worshipped, and celebrated Christmas, on what for many hundreds of years was an island, the Isle of Ely. In the year AD 673, Queen Etheldreda founded a monastic house there for both monks and nuns and became their first abbess. She renounced all the luxury she was born to and lived an austere, strict and cloistered life. There is a legend which says that monks from the rival Abbey of Ramsey used to take advantage of

Madonna and Child by Masaccio, 1426

the Fenland mists to break in and carry away sacred relics from under the noses of the Ely monks.

And now I am trying to find my way to Ely through sinister swirls of the same mists. For more than 800 years the great cathedral of Ely has been visible for miles. But not tonight. I am going to be very late. I should definitely have got up earlier for this journey. St Etheldreda's strict rule would have accepted no excuses for my lateness, but St Benedict would have been a little kinder:

When they rise for the work of God, let them gently encourage one another, on account of the excuses to which the sleepy are addicted.

Five minutes before the recording is due to begin, I reach a junction. At last, Ely is signposted – in both directions. It is time to replace panic with prayer. St Ambrose comes to my aid:

Thy cradle here shall glitter bright, and darkness glow with new-born light, no more shall night extinguish day, where love's bright beams their power display.

And, like a miracle, Ely Cathedral is suddenly visible, its famous Octagon Lantern tower lit up in a night sky free from mist and filled once more with 'broken-off bits of heaven'.

O Jesu, virgin-born to thee eternal praise and glory be, when with the Father we adore and Holy Spirit, evermore.

In the city the streets are deserted except for the huge, quietly humming vehicles of the BBC Outside Broadcast unit. Everyone else is in the cathedral, holding candles and singing one of the nation's favourite carols. At the very heart of the cathedral is a 'living' nativity scene, depicted by children from the junior school at the King's School Ely. In the thirteenth century, St Francis of Assisi spoke of Christ as 'the little brother of all mankind' and encouraged Christians to make their own 'pilgrimage of the heart' to Bethlehem. On one Christmas Eve, St Francis created just such a tableau:

He had a manger prepared, hay carried in and an ox and an ass led to the spot. The brothers are summoned, the people arrive, the forest amplifies with their cries, and that venerable night is rendered bright and solemn by a multitude of bright lights and by resonant and harmonious hymns of praise. God stands before the manger, filled with piety, bathed in tears and overcome with joy.
ST BONAVENTURE

Tonight in Ely it feels as though God has changed his mind again. At Christmas the stars do come down to earth. We are all blessed.

Away in a manger

9

When *Songs of Praise* showed a whole programme about a nativity play recently, I was glad to be watching on my own, peering through tear-filled eyes, and trying not to embarrass the cat and dog with my sobs. Brought up in an age in which men were not expected to show emotion, I learned as an adult that it is usually better not to attend a nativity play if you don't want to 'let the side down'. This little scene, acted out annually by small thespians dressed in old dressing-gowns and bits of curtain and clutching toy lambs and a doll, is enough to reduce anybody to a red-eyed wreck. And, of course, nobody must be left out. Donald Reeves, former Rector of St James's, Piccadilly, remembers being dressed up as a crocodile in a stuffy green costume for his primary school nativity play. His mother or teacher must have been thinking of *Peter Pan*. Even the legend of St Francis of Assisi's open-air nativity with live animals, a format much copied today, never included large reptiles as far as I know.

'Away in a manger' is a children's carol for us all. We watch as the angels, the shepherds and the children dressed as sheep are coaxed into place. The inn keeper and Joseph are restrained from overdoing their roles, the three wise men make their solemn entrance offering silver-paper-covered boxes labelled gold, frankincense and myrrh, and Mary collects them on her baby's behalf, like a lady-in-waiting to the Queen on a royal walkabout. And eventually we come to the big finale. We look on as what old pantomime programmes described as 'The Entire Company' creates a tableau as solemn and dignified as a medieval painting. And of course we all want to join in with their last big number. As we sing through our tears, 'Away in a manger' has become the one carol of which it can truly be said that we know the words 'by heart'.

One way to ensure a tear-free experience of a nativity play is to be responsible for filming it. My first experience of filming a village school nativity for *Songs of Praise* nearly came to grief when Mary was suddenly very sick. She refused to allow an understudy to step in, so we had to wait patiently for her to recover. The teacher calmed everyone down by reading aloud the story of the birth of Jesus from Luke's Gospel. Once Mary was able to rejoin us and the traditional tableau was formed, the choir of Clare College, Cambridge, sang 'Away in a manger' using the Sir David Willcocks setting of the familiar tune, with a solo voice singing the last verse while the choir hummed. It was extraordinary and beautiful, but somehow not nearly as tear-inducing as the local amateur sing-a-long.

We may never know who really wrote this carol. Rather oddly, it has been wrongly attributed to the great sixteenth-century architect of the Reformation, Martin Luther. Luther, who renounced his priestly vows and married later in life, was said to have written it for his children. He *did* write a nativity hymn for his children, however, which begins: 'Give heed, my heart, lift up thine eyes: Who is it in yon manger lies?'

Verse 2 sounds more like the work of a man who stood alone for his faith against princes and popes. He set this verse for the solo voice of an angel:

Welcome to earth, thou noble Guest,
Through whom even wicked men are blest!
Thou com'st to share our misery;
What can we render, Lord to thee?

The rather less exciting explanation is that the gentle words of 'Away in a manger' were written anonymously in America in 1883 on an occasion to celebrate the 400th anniversary of Luther's birth. Originally there were only two verses. Then at the beginning of the twentieth century an American Methodist Sunday school teacher, John McFarland, wrote a final verse which is quite different in tone, and moves away from describing the scene to words of prayer for the singer.

The words are traditionally set to the tune

Away in a manger, no crib for a bed,
the little Lord Jesus laid down his sweet head;
the stars in the bright sky looked down where he lay –
the little Lord Jesus, asleep on the hay.

The cattle are lowing, the baby awakes,
but little Lord Jesus, no crying he makes.
I love thee, Lord Jesus! Look down from the sky,
and stay by my side until morning is nigh.

Be near me, Lord Jesus: I ask thee to stay
close by me for ever, and love me, I pray;
bless all the dear children in thy tender care,
and fit us for heaven to live with thee there.

'Cradle Song' by William Kirkpatrick, who also wrote many gospel songs. If you were watching the 2004 Christmas *Songs of Praise* from Ely Cathedral, you may have heard, very briefly, the choir singing the familiar words to a different tune, 'Normandy' by Edgar Pettman.

As a child, I never took part in a nativity play – I was far too nervous and self-conscious to stand on a stage – but I did get to know the words of 'Away in a manger' as a radio listener. They were sung in the utterly unique style of the Luton Girls' Choir, which was very popular in the 1940s, and broadcast on what was then the BBC *Light Programme*. The choir called the carol 'The holy child', and the tune they used was by Easthope Martin, a rather obscure English composer who was better known for writing the popular song 'Come to the fair', and for promoting the pianolo, that well-known feature of the Edwardian parlour.

The founder and conductor of the Luton Girls' Choir, Arthur Davies, was a strict disciplinarian, and only unmarried girls under the age of 23 who lived within 5 miles of Luton were allowed to join. Davies helped the choir to perfect an amazing diction, and had they performed on TV the words would not have needed to be shown on-screen. The choir decided never to sing again after their authoritarian conductor died in 1977, but I can still remember the sound of them singing the carol, which I first heard in Christmas 1948.

Even though this carol has no direct link with Martin Luther, it does, in its simple way, perfectly fit his view of music:

Beside theology, music is the only art capable of affording peace and joy of the heart…
A proof of this is that the devil, the originator of sorrowful anxieties and restless troubles, flees before the sound of music almost as much as before the Word of God.

'Away in a manger' sung at a nativity play is not only a reminder of the past and of childhood, but it is also Christmas Present, to all of us, from the children. Seen on TV against the backdrop of cruel news images created by the grown-up world, we know that we, like Scrooge, are all being given one more chance. No wonder we cry.

Christians, awake

<u>15</u>

If, like me, you enjoy watching old British comedy films, you will remember the *Belles of St Trinian's* and the masterclass performances by Alastair Sim as the world's most eccentric and incompetent headmistress. I was fascinated to discover recently that this distinguished comic actor used to provide elocution and presentation tutorials for Church of Scotland ministers in training. I have also found out that there was an actual school called St Trinian's in Edinburgh, on which Ronald Searle's

Belles of St Trinian's, starring Alastair Sim and George Cole (1954)

original story was based – and I have even met a St Trinian's Old Girl.

One of the fictional St Trinian's headmistress's more dubious collaborators was 'Flash Harry', played by George Cole, whose louche entrances from his secret lair somewhere in the school grounds were always accompanied by music, composed by Malcolm Arnold, that brilliantly captured his air of jaunty craftiness. The appearance of Flash Harry makes a perfect introduction to John Byrom, author of 'Christians, awake', who in an eighteenth-century account was described this way:

He carried a stick with a crook-top, and wore a curious, low-polled, slouched hat, from under the long-peaked brim of which his face bent forward a cautiously inquisitive kind of look, as if he were in the habit of prying into everything, without caring to let everything enter deeply into him.

John Byrom

John Byrom was born in Manchester in 1691, and after first studying medicine in France he made an astonishing change of direction by first inventing, and then teaching, the art of writing in shorthand. One of the earliest beneficiaries of this new skill was a friend of Byrom's, Charles Wesley, who recorded his journeys in shorthand and composed many of his hymns this way, even while riding on horseback. If it is true that Wesley wrote 6,500 hymns, then the newly invented shorthand must have been a great boon.

Byrom was also a respected poet, and his great hymn 'Christians, awake' first appeared as a poem – a present for his daughter, Dolly, which she found by her place at breakfast on Christmas morning 1749. It was rather longer than the version we sing, and I wonder whether the opening of other presents stopped while it was read aloud, its final, hopeful lines setting the scene for the Christmas feast.

A year later, Byrom himself woke on Christmas Eve to hear 'angelic hosts' outside his bedroom window. His friend John Wainwright, the organist, had borrowed the poem from Dolly and set it to the tune that is sung today, which is sometimes called 'Yorkshire' and sometimes 'Stockport'. To deliver his Christmas gift, Wainwright brought the entire choir from Manchester Parish Church to sing the hymn outside Byrom's window. The following day – Christmas Day 1750 – the hymn was sung for the first time in Stockport Parish Church.

More than 200 years later, I was sent by the BBC as a very raw, new producer to look after all religious programmes coming from the North of England. I knew almost nothing at all about the area except that I associated 'Christians, awake' with Stockport. When – soon after I arrived – I was asked to set up a Christmas Day broadcast, I thought that there was only one place to choose. At the

Christians, awake, salute the happy morn
whereon the Saviour of the world was
  born;
rise to adore the mystery of love,
which hosts of angels chanted from
  above;
with them the joyful tidings first begun
of God incarnate and the Virgin's Son.

Then to the watchful shepherds it was
  told,
who heard the angelic herald's voice,
  'Behold,
I bring good tidings of a Saviour's birth
to you and all the nations upon earth;
this day hath God fulfilled his promised
  word,
this day is born a Saviour, Christ the
  Lord.'

He spake; and straightway the celestial
  choir
in hymns of joy, unknown before,
  conspire.
The praises of redeeming love they sang,
and heaven's whole orb with hallelujahs
  rang;
God's highest glory was their anthem
  still,
peace upon earth, from each to each good
  will.

Then Bethl'em straight the enlightened
  shepherds sought
to see the wonder God for us had
  wrought.
They saw their Saviour as the angel said,
the swaddled infant in the manger laid.
They to their flocks and praising God
  return
with joyful hearts that did within them
  burn.

Like Mary, let us ponder in our mind
God's wondrous love in saving
  humankind.
Trace we the babe, who has retrieved our
  loss,
from his poor manger to his bitter cross.
Tread in his steps, assisted by his grace,
till our first heavenly state again takes
  place.

Then may we hope, the angelic thrones
  among,
to sing, redeemed, a glad triumphal song.
He that was born upon this joyful day
around us all his glory shall display;
saved by his love, incessant we shall sing
the eternal praise of heaven's almighty
  King.

time, the vicar of St George's Parish Church was Wilfred Garlick. Over the years he had become a radio celebrity for his broadcasts called *The Parson Calls*. This programme used a popular form to deal with what John Byrom would have called 'theological

enquiry', so I thought that I had hit on a brilliant idea.

Wilfred Garlick sounded kindly but gruff when I telephoned. After receiving a few minutes of my waffle in silence, he interrupted to say, 'All right, young man, but you are not getting "Christians, awake" at any price!' I did not know then what the distinguished expert on hymnody, Erik Routley, reported: that there was still a folk custom around Stockport of 'singing the hymn in the small hours of Christmas morning'. I can well imagine that not all versions of the carol sung outside the vicarage had been as harmonious as its première outside the composer's home in 1750.

In fact, Manchester, home today of the *Songs of Praise* programme team, would have been quite a dangerous place to live in Byrom's time. During the Jacobite Rebellion of 1745, while his friends John and Charles Wesley had kept their heads down, John Byrom declared himself for Bonnie Prince Charlie. He even produced a satirical verse worthy of today's *Private Eye* magazine:

God bless the King – I mean the faith's
  defender;
God bless – no harm in blessing – the
  Pretender;
But who Pretender is, and who is King,
God bless us all – that's quite another thing.

On 28 November 1745, Manchester was invaded by the rebel army, who set about recruiting volunteers to join them on their march on London. The *London Magazine* reported that 'several papists' took five guineas and were given a white cockade to wear, but that almost no one else from the region signed up. The rebels mugged passers-by, seizing all 'ready cash', and then departed after one uproarious night of plunder.

On 10 December, they were back and in retreat, but they once more seized everything they could lay hands on. In those days, there were only two constables to look after the whole of Manchester. If John Byrom was at home it would have been a time for keeping his head well down – like Flash Harry in St Trinian's – under the slouched hat, with or without the white cockade. Byrom wrote his hymn when peace had been restored, but those events, which must still have been fresh in the public mind, give new meaning to the salutation of 'the happy morn'.

'Christians, awake' is not sung very often on *Songs of Praise*, so I hope its inclusion in the nation's favourite carol poll will prompt another performance soon. Having failed with Wilfred Garlick, I was happy to include it in a special 1978 Christmas *Songs of Praise*, sung by massed choirs of nurses and doctors and a capacity audience in the Festival Hall in London. Coaxed on by ranks of fanfare trumpeters and the organ with all stops out, everyone roared out the hymn. I hope that the performance did justice to Byrom and his friend, John Wainwright. Writing in the 1750s, John Wesley advised:

Sing All. Sing lustily and with good courage. Beware of singing as if you were half dead, or half asleep. Sing modestly. Do not bawl, and sing in time.

Now we know what to expect on *Songs of Praise*.

God rest you merry, gentlemen
(English traditional carol)

16

Foggier yet, and colder. Piercing, searching, biting cold. If the good Saint Dunstan had but nipped the Evil Spirit's nose with a touch of such weather as that instead of using his familiar weapons, then indeed he would have roared to lusty purpose. The owner of one scant young nose, gnawed and mumbled by the hungry cold as bones are gnawed by dogs, stooped down at Scrooge's keyhole to regale him with a Christmas carol: but at the first sound of:

'God bless you, merry gentleman!
May nothing you dismay!'

Scrooge seized the ruler with such energy of action that the singer fled in terror, leaving the keyhole to the fog and even more congenial frost.

A Christmas Carol, the first of a number of Christmas books written by Charles Dickens, went on sale on 19 December 1843. The tale of the mean old miser, Scrooge – who renounces his ways after spending a long Christmas night being haunted by spirits of his past, present and future who show him visions of the consequences of his wrongdoing – was not only an instant hit with readers, but was described by another author, William Thackeray, as a 'national benefit'.

Dickens wrote *A Christmas Carol* very quickly in the months leading up to Christmas. He was an adviser to the extraordinary Victorian philanthropist, Angela Burdett-Coutts, whose influence ranged from providing hundreds of Christmas feasts for London's poor to the construction of churches and whole housing estates. One of Dickens's duties was to weed out the fraudsters and scrooges who clamoured for Miss Coutts's charity.

Even in those days, London's shops were filled for weeks with glittering seasonal trinkets, but the author was also aware of the nearby world of grinding poverty. Setting the scene for his famous story about charity and generosity finally overcoming self-centred meanness, Dickens used the opening lines of a popular Christmas ballad that would have been frequently heard on the streets of London in the eighteenth and nineteenth centuries. His 1843 quote differs slightly from the version we sing today, which was published in 1871. He replaces 'rest' with 'bless',

The Nativity by Ottaviano di Martino Nelli (1424)

perhaps because he knew that in the original the word 'rest' meant 'keep'.

To get to the bottom of the story, we have to go back as far as 1770, to a collection of songs called the 'Roxburgh Ballads'. These ballads were part of the popular sheet music industry, which set in song stories that had gripped the public imagination, and sold them on the streets of London. In this case, the carol seems at first to be based simply on Luke's version of the Christmas story and the shepherds visiting the manger, but

there is also a more surprising link with an earthquake in London – as Pam Rhodes hinted to *Songs of Praise* viewers when she introduced the carol in the 2004 *Songs of Praise* 'Big Sing' from the Albert Hall.

Although for us today it seems an unlikely part of London life, there really were two earthquakes in the capital during Queen Elizabeth I's reign, and both were on Christmas Eve. In 1750 there were several more tremors. In his account, written in 1773, John Noorthouck reports that at

lunchtime on 8 February 1750, 'chairs shaking in the houses and the brass and pewter rattling on the shelves' led to widespread panic. Everyone attending a meeting in Westminster Hall 'expected the building would be demolished', while in the suburbs, church bells jangled uncontrollably.

After three different tremors, a religious fanatic stirred up further panic by circulating 'scandalous whispers', claiming to know when a fourth and greater earthquake was due. He gained much credibility from a letter circulating on the streets from the Bishop of London which said that it was 'every man's duty to give attention to all the warnings which God in his mercy affords to a sinful people'. The bishop 'lamented the general depravity of the times, the horrid oaths and blasphemies, the detestable lewdness and impiety, luxury and love of pleasure that prevailed'.

When nothing further happened, the 'prophet', who had been making money selling 'cards and wax candles', was 'sent to a madhouse'. The bishop, of course, survived. But this carol could well have been written as a calming reminder for very nervous people of the saving event in the stable at Bethlehem.

The version that Dickens knew, long after the earthquake scare had been forgotten, offered good news in a London of impenetrable fogs, dimly lit streets and dark, spooky alleys. Dickens saw Christmas as a time not for religious fervour but for families gathered at the fireside, telling one another ghost stories and singing songs full of good cheer. In the *Pickwick Papers* the author describes just such a Christmas Eve at Mr Wardle's, with much joyful toasting of the company encouraged by all sharing the mighty bowl of deep, rich wassail:

'This' said Mr Pickwick, looking around him, 'this is indeed comfort.' 'Our invariable custom,' replied Mr Wardle. 'Everybody sits down with us on Christmas Eve – servants and all; and here we wait, until the clock strikes twelve, to usher Christmas in, and beguile the time with forfeits and old stories.'

PICKWICK PAPERS

God rest you merry, gentlemen,
let nothing you dismay,
for Jesus Christ our Saviour
was born upon this day,
to save us all from Satan's power
when we were gone astray.

O tidings of comfort and joy,
  comfort and joy!
O tidings of comfort and joy!

In Bethlehem in Jewry
this blessèd babe was born,
and laid within a manger
upon this blessèd morn;
the which his mother Mary
nothing did take in scorn.

From God our heavenly Father
a blessèd angel came;
and unto certain shepherds
brought tidings of the same,
how that in Bethlehem was born
the Son of God by name:

The shepherds at those tidings
rejoicèd much in mind
and left their flocks a-feeding
in tempest, storm and wind,
and went to Bethlehem straightway
this blessèd babe to find.

But when to Bethlehem they came,
whereat this infant lay,
they found him in a manger
where oxen feed on hay;
his mother Mary, kneeling,
unto the Lord did pray:

Now to the Lord sing praises,
all you within this place,
and with true love and brotherhood
each other now embrace.
The holy tide of Christmas
all others doth efface.

The first known Christmas card, created for Sir Henry Cole by John C. Horsley in 1845

As the years have passed, the words have been altered. Jesus, born 'to save us all from Satan's power when we were gone astray' has replaced Jesus, the Saviour born 'so frequently to vanquish all the friends [or fiends] of Satan quiet'. The *Oxford Book of Carols*, first published in 1928, has an eight-verse version sung to what is called the 'London' tune. The last verse begins, 'God bless the ruler of this house, and send him long to reign...'

I have often wondered who the 'ruler' is. A Victorian father, or a Georgian king? Just before Christmas Eve 2004, I found myself singing the carol in a cathedral somewhere in Britain. Right behind me, thankful no doubt to escape from the tabloid journalists who are not normally found at such events, was a member of the Cabinet. He was completely silent until we all stood to sing 'God rest you merry, gentlemen', when, in a strong baritone voice, he belted out every verse before falling completely silent again. I am sure Mr Pickwick – also known as the late and much-loved star of the musical and *Songs of Praise* presenter, Sir Harry Secombe – would have approved.

Good King Wenceslas

20

The Boxing Day service seemed to be going quite well. The vicar had preached a thoughtful sermon on the theme of the carol, 'When a child is born', and then 'Good King Wenceslas' was announced. While we all rummaged through our hymn books to find it – or rather not to find it because it turned out it was on a separate sheet – most of us had already begun singing the familiar words, which we all knew by heart. In fact not just most of us – everyone. Everyone, that is, except the vicar. He stood emanating disapproval, looking out at us with a grim expression, his mouth firmly closed right to the very last note.

Having thoroughly enjoyed singing the familiar tale, in spite of having been rather unnerved by the vicar, I went home and read that the words of 'Good King Wenceslas' were described as 'colourful but dodgy' in a music magazine's Christmas carol feature. Then I came across a rather solemn review of hymns, written forty years ago, where the eminent writer, also a vicar, left all thoughts of charity behind:

John Mason Neale

I hope the day is not far distant when good King Wenceslas will catch pneumonia and die from over-exposure. He has been looking out of the window far too long.

The clergy generally do not seem to like this story of the king and his page boy – perhaps because it is not based on any of the gospel stories of the nativity, and indeed does not appear to have any scriptural connections at all. Yet it was written by a remarkable Victorian clergyman to whom we owe some of the finest translations into English of hymns from the earliest days of the church.

John Mason Neale was never afraid of controversy. He stood against his bishops in his search for the numinous through candles, incense and altar crosses at a time when strict puritan austerity prevailed. He was immensely erudite and began a correspondence with the Orthodox Church, introducing elements from their Eastern tradition that are still found in Anglican churches today. He could understand and speak twenty languages, including Latin and Greek. It is to Neale that we owe such familiar and well-loved hymns as 'Jerusalem the golden' and 'The day of resurrection'. Yet in the material world Neale was not successful. Briefly vicar of Crawley in Sussex after his ordination, he spent most of his life as the poorly paid warden of Sackville College in East Grinstead. Everything he did in the college chapel incurred the displeasure of Bishop Gilbert of Chichester, and he was forbidden to practise his vocation. It is like a story from Trollope's *Barchester Chronicles*.

In 1850 he was invited to become the Provost of St Ninian's in Perth, the first cathedral to be built north of the border since the Reformation. Neale travelled to

Good King Wenceslas by Anne Anderson

Scotland on the newly built railway, but it is said that he found the climate too cold, and although he devised a great service for the consecration of the cathedral, almost immediately afterwards he returned to Sussex, living in obscurity until in 1853 he produced his very successful *Carols for Christmas and Easter*. This little volume was to have an immense effect on the place of carol-singing in the churches, and influenced both the *Cowley Carol Book* and the *Oxford Book of Carols* almost 50 years later. Here are riches galore for those who tire of the endless recycling of familiar carols, blasting out day and night from early autumn onwards in supermarkets and chain stores.

Neale took a tune that originally belonged to a hymn for spring called 'Flower carol', taken from *Piae Cantiones*, a sixteenth-century collection of devotional music from Sweden and Germany, and set it to the legend of the tenth-century King Wenceslas. The story had come to Neale's notice through his correspondence with the Eastern European Orthodox church. The old ruler of Bohemia, who became its patron saint after his martyrdom, was later to become the symbol of Czech independence.

'Good King Wenceslas' tells the story of one man's piety and generous self-sacrifice and is intended to inspire charity in others. On a cold winter night the day after Christmas – the anniversary of the death of Stephen, the first Christian martyr – a king and his young page boy set off to visit a poor peasant, taking him logs for his fire and food to eat. I am not sure what the significance of St Agnes and her fountain is, but the scenery makes me wonder whether Neale might have been remembering his brief sojourn in Perthshire when he wrote

this carol. North of Perth, 'a good league hence', the traveller finds himself in the Highlands of Scotland where there are mountains and forests and the winters are bitter; and, in the nineteenth century at least, the lairds would certainly have needed their consciences stirred to wade through rude winds into a dark and snowy night to seek out the poor and needy. The squires of Victorian Sussex were undoubtedly no more generous, but the surrounding countryside was less rugged.

In 1979, in a Christmas *Songs of Praise* spectacular from the Royal Festival Hall, I directed the cameras as a great choir of nurses and doctors from all the London hospitals, and a capacity audience, had much fun singing 'Good King Wenceslas'. Under the conductor, Charles Farncombe, and assisted by the late James Blades, one of the world's greatest timpanists, the audience was asked both to sing and to provide appropriate wintry sound effects. As 'the wind blew stronger', the audience whistled and wailed mightily, while the king and his page's footsteps were marked by clog-like sounds on the drums and cymbals, played by James Blades. To add to the pantomime atmosphere, during rehearsals Blades kept producing illicit drum rolls every time the conductor turned his back on him.

For the final performance of 'Good King Wenceslas', choir and audience together were equally energetic and wild – some people persisting in giving loud wolf-whistles throughout – yet at the same time it was oddly moving. By taking part everyone was performing an act of charity, raising money for the Malcolm Sargent Cancer Fund, set up to remember another flamboyant conductor who had popularised many lesser-known but beautiful carols by introducing them into his concerts. As I watched the shots, I was thinking of a brave, desperately ill, little boy whom we had filmed for *Songs of Praise*, talking to Leonard Pearcy in the Great Ormond Street Hospital for sick children. His fight for life was being helped by the Malcolm Sargent charity, and he expressed a wish, at Christmas-time, for health and happiness for everyone. Together, this little boy and Sir Malcolm somehow fitted perfectly into John Mason Neale's carol about a young page and an old king, with their final words to us all:

Ye who now will bless the poor,
shall yourselves find blessing.

Good King Wenceslas looked out
on the feast of Stephen,
when the snow lay round about,
deep and crisp and even;
brightly shone the moon that night,
though the frost was cruel,
when a poor man came in sight,
gathering winter fuel.

'Hither, page, and stand by me;
if thou know'st it, telling –
yonder peasant, who is he?
Where and what his dwelling?'
'Sire, he lives a good league hence,
underneath the mountain,
right against the forest fence,
by Saint Agnes' fountain.'

'Bring me flesh, and bring me wine!
Bring me pine logs hither!
Thou and I will see him dine
when we bear them thither.'
Page and monarch forth they went,
forth they went together,
through the rude wind's wild lament
and the bitter weather.

'Sire, the night is darker now,
and the wind blows stronger;
fails my heart, I know not how,
I can go no longer.'
'Mark my footsteps, good my page,
tread thou in them boldly:
thou shalt find the winter's rage
freeze thy blood less coldly.'

In his master's steps he trod,
where the snow lay dinted;
heat was in the very sod
which the saint had printed.
Therefore, Christian men, be sure,
wealth or rank possessing,
ye who now will bless the poor
shall yourselves find blessing.

Hark! the herald-angels sing

3

When 'Hark! the herald-angels sing' is announced at the carol service, we all know what to expect: trumpets, drums and a demonstration of the organist's formidable ability to pull out all the stops at once. When everyone stands to sing what the Edwardian churchman, Percy Dearmer, called 'the most popular English hymn in the world', we seem to be celebrating not only Christmas but also the greatest of all hymn writers, Charles Wesley.

Yet if we were faithful to the hymn exactly as Wesley wrote it in 1743, we would begin with two strangely different lines:

Hark, how all the welkin rings,
Glory to the king of kings…

I like the word 'welkin', which is given three meanings by the *Oxford English Dictionary*. It is 'the arch or vault of heaven overhead; the region of the air in which the clouds float and birds fly; a cloud'.

As we leave the midnight service at St Mary's Episcopal Cathedral in Edinburgh, Christmas Day begins. There is a warm,

Charles Wesley

gusty wind and the upward glow from floodlit buildings is reflected in a few scudding clouds. The streets are empty and the rest of the world seems asleep. Soon we are out in unlit countryside and millions of stars can be seen shining above us. In this starlit silence of the 'welkin', I can almost hear the sound of angels celebrating Christmas with everything that God has created.

During summer holidays spent on the beach, my mother would try hard to interest her two young sons in nature rather than passing warships by getting us to hunt for cowrie shells to take back to the suburbs. Once home, if we pressed the shell against our ears we would hear again the sound of the faraway sea. I thought of it as the sound of heaven. So I like to celebrate Christmas with Wesley's 'welkin', and one of my mother's favourite cowrie shells is beside me as I write.

The final version of 'Hark! the herald-angels sing' is the result of much pruning and editing by two of Charles Wesley's colleagues. Martin Madan was a lawyer, who later became Chaplain to the Lock Hospital,

Hark! the herald-angels sing
glory to the new-born King,
peace on earth, and mercy mild,
God and sinners reconciled.
Joyful, all ye nations rise,
join the triumph of the skies;
with the angelic host proclaim,
'Christ is born in Bethlehem.'

Hark! the herald-angels sing
Glory to the new-born King.

Christ, by highest heaven adored,
Christ, the everlasting Lord,
late in time behold him come,
offspring of a virgin's womb.
Veiled in flesh the Godhead see!
Hail, the incarnate deity!
Pleased as man with man to dwell,
Jesus, our Emmanuel.

Hail, the heaven-born Prince of peace!
Hail, the sun of righteousness!
Light and life to all he brings,
risen with healing in his wings,
mild he lays his glory by,
born that man no more may die,
born to raise the sons of earth,
born to give them second birth.

one of London's largest orphanages. The children were taught to sing and gave annual charity concerts before huge audiences. They would certainly have been asked to appear on *Songs of Praise*.

Madan altered many of Wesley's original words, sometimes to the author's irritation. For example, in the carol Madan changed two lines: 'Universal nature say, "Christ the Lord is born today"' became the familiar 'With the angelic host proclaim, "Christ is born in Bethlehem."'

The opening words, 'Hark! the herald-angels sing', were supplied by another of John and Charles Wesley's colleagues, George Whitefield. Like the Wesleys, his religious experience took him out of the Anglican Church and he became a fiery preacher, always creating a wild fervour among the huge crowds that came to hear him. Travelling to America in 1740, Whitefield came under the influence of another evangelist, Jonathan Edwards. As an uncompromising Calvinist, Edwards did not accept the Wesleys' teaching that the grace of God was freely available to 'sheep' and 'goats' alike. For Whitefield the goats were forever separated from the sheep. As a result, Whitefield and the Wesleys parted company so dramatically that the whole Methodist movement split into two.

Some hymn books still print a fourth verse of the hymn in which Charles Wesley's theology of free grace is spelled out, as the singer invites Christ to live in their heart:

Come, Desire of nations come,
fix in us thy humble home;
rise, the woman's conquering Seed,
bruise in us the serpent's head;
now display thy saving power,
ruined nature now restore,
now in mystic union join
thine to ours, and ours to thine.

This verse has never been included when sung on *Songs of Praise*, but I wonder if it was included in a wartime Christmas service described in the diary of the late John Hayter, an Anglican priest who as a young man was interned by the Japanese during the four dreadful years of the occupation of Singapore. Hayter, a remarkable preacher and much-loved vicar in the New Forest, was a chaplain during the Second World War, imprisoned with his bishop, Leonard Wilson. He always shared Bishop Wilson's conviction that even the most evil of enemies must be forgiven, although he himself never had to suffer torture as the bishop did.

On the first Christmas Day of the occupation, the Japanese for once allowed separated husbands and wives to meet at the cathedral where the annual service of Nine Lessons and Carols was being held – in which Charles Wesley's hymn was included. There was such a great number present that many were crowded two or three deep in front of the altar. Hayter wrote in his diary, 'In the middle by chance was Alexander, the Bishop's Indian Secretary, his wife beside him holding their baby in her arms. It was a perfect nativity tableau. With the carols and hymns sung in seven different languages, it was a stupendous occasion!'

Christmas Day in Changi jail, later on during the war, was a much grimmer affair. Hayter likened the service he held in secret in his cell to the experience of the first-century Christians as they worshipped in the catacombs of Rome. Bishop Wilson celebrated communion in another cell with just a few grains of cooked rice instead of bread and some water instead of wine, which he passed through the bars to fellow prisoners on their knees. 'The spirit of Christmas was in that prison,' wrote Hayter.

From their cells, the prisoners could see the sky and the tower of the Methodist Church, a glimpse of the 'welkin'. During his worst hours of torture, Bishop Wilson used to pray using the words of another Wesley hymn that he could remember, 'Christ whose glory fills the sky'. His torturers asked him if he still believed in God. The bishop said that, with God's help, he did.

'Then why does not God save you?' shouted the torturer.

'He does,' the Bishop managed to answer, 'but not from pain. He saves me by giving me the spirit to bear it.'

In dulci jubilo

19

The nation's favourite top twenty carols contain only one that is written in what musicologists describe as 'macaronic' form. This extraordinary term is apparently derived from the pasta macaroni because, like layers of complementary food ingredients, macaronic songs interleave two different languages. 'Ding-dong merrily on high', 'Shepherds in the fields abiding' and 'In dulci jubilo' all mix English and Latin. So perhaps 'macaronic' is a medieval term for 'franglais'.

Perhaps if you are a lawyer, or remember your Latin from schooldays rather better than I do, you will have no difficulty with the movement from one language to another found within each verse of prayerful devotion. I doubt that many of us would claim to understand the literal meaning of all the words as we sing 'In dulci jubilo', but its message of wistful longing for reprieve from sadness is clear enough. It expresses a yearning not only to be present in the stable – 'O that we were there' – but for the presence of Jesus in our lives here and now.

In its original fourteenth-century form, this carol was not written in English and Latin but in German and Latin. The third verse, 'O Patris caritas' (O love of the Father), has been attributed to Martin Luther. In 1540, less than half a century after the word 'carol' had itself entered the English language, the German words were translated into English by John Wedderburn for use in his collection *Gude and Godly Ballates* (Good and Godly Ballads).

The *Oxford Book of Carols* translates 'In dulci jubilo' as 'in sweet shouting' or 'in jubilation'. 'Sweet shouting' may be literally correct, but it sounds like an effect that conductor Paul Leddington Wright would not welcome at the *Songs of Praise* 'Big Sing' of the nation's favourite carols.

The next line of Latin not only takes us to a Bethlehem stable 2,000 years ago, but also introduces a tradition still familiar throughout Europe today. *In praesepio* means 'in a manger', and no Italian will be unfamiliar with the beautiful *presepe* – the nativity scenes on display in their homes and in shops and halls in their villages, towns and cities. Since the eighteenth century, Italians have competed to build ever larger and more beautiful *presepe*, which are displayed from 6 December until Epiphany on 6 January when the figures of the wise men and their gifts complete the scene and, by tradition, children receive presents too.

In Italy the *presepio* is far more important than the Christmas tree, but even in Austria, where the tree (the *tannenbaum*) is welcomed in song, elaborate manger scenes are also much admired. One such display, first shown

Nativity scene from the Christmas crib built in the eighteenth century for King Charles III of Naples

in 1955, has grown to feature no fewer than 778 model figures around the manger. Another – the 'mechanical' manger – has 300 figures that move to the musical accompaniment of a Bohemian cylinder organ.

But the place to see the very best *presepio* is in Naples, where each year new figures depict celebrities and politicians in the news. Recently the Italian Prime Minister, Sylvio Berlusconi, has appeared in model form. However, unlike the recent upset in England surrounding a waxwork display of the holy family that used the faces of David and Victoria Beckham and the American President, George W. Bush, any celebrity featuring in the *presepio* is always confined to the role of a mere on-looker. The very heart of the scene is traditional and is an object of great reverence. Families gather together every morning to pray in front of their *presepio*.

Our own *presepio* appears each December. My wife Liz has had the same little manger scene since childhood. It is small and rather battered now, and its singed straw roof bears witness to the candles lit in front of it each Christmas Eve. For years the chipped figures of Joseph and Mary were joined by a diminishing selection of ageing sheep and a three-legged donkey. Then one December I came home, proudly bearing a complete, new set of figures from Peru. Liz pointed to where her own fine, new set of shepherds, wise men and animals were, purchased that same day and all ready to be put in place. So now, by the time we reach Epiphany, Jesus and the three-legged donkey are barely visible among the great crowd of sheep, oxen, shepherds and wise men, all jostling for space.

'In dulci jubilo', with its fourteenth-century tune harmonised by Robert Pearsall – an English barrister who became a musician and worked in Germany in the early nineteenth century – is best sung or listened to while looking at even the simplest *presepio*. As I have unravelled a little of the history of Christmas customs in Naples, and visited their welcome pages on the world wide web, I have come across a new computer experience of 'macaronic' language. Here is how we are introduced to the *presepio*:

The little figures pay some of ventiquattro centuries ago were said cram votive.

I do get the point. I think. It means 'O that we were there.'

In dulci jubilo
Now sing we all i-o, i-o,
He, our love, our pleasure
Lies in praesepio,
Like brightly gleaming
   treasure
Matris in gremio:
Alpha es et O!
Alpha es et O!

O Jesu parvule,
for you I long alway;
hear me in my sadness,
O puer optime;
With goodness and with
   gladness,
O princeps gloriae,
trahe me post te!
trahe me post te!

O Patris caritas!
O Nati lenitas!
We were past reprieving
per nostra crimina;
for us you are retrieving
coelorum gaudia:
O that we were there!
O that we were there!

Ubi sunt gaudia?
O nowhere more than there;
angels there are singing
nova cantica,
And there the bells are
   ringing
in regis curia,
O that we were there!
O that we were there!

In the bleak mid-winter

1

The air is very still, and the water in the ditch that stretches away into a murky horizon is as black as the sky in the flat landscape. Around the fields and beside the paths, patches of tired snow remain in dirty heaps, petrified by the hard frost. The world is black and white. The scene is unravelling and repeating itself on a long winter's train journey across England. As we cross over deserted lanes, every feature of the landscape seems to be at right angles to the journey I am making. A small cottage has unlit windows as black as the sky; the fields are empty.

It is this cold, colourless landscape that is the setting of the nation's favourite carol. What is it about this bleak picture that attracts so many people? I know that for me it is a scene that feels almost holy, where I can be alone with my thoughts.

It is difficult to film this sort of experience. Even when the frosty scene is before them, *Songs of Praise* directors usually have to use crafty filters to recreate the strange resonance of a bleak, mid-winter landscape. Often, while making *Songs of Praise* films on a winter's day, I have had to give up; it becomes too dark to get an exposure, the camera man shakes his head and I am reminded of my own childhood attempts to use my Box Brownie anywhere where the sun was not shining. 'It'll be a waste,' my father used to say. 'It won't come out.'

Only once, long ago in 1978, did I manage to capture on film the numinous image of winter that the poet Christina Rossetti evoked in her carol. It was at a special Christmas *Songs of Praise*, which brought together a huge heart-warming charity carol concert in the Royal Festival Hall and a simple Christmas service in the small Suffolk village of Clare. While we were filming in Clare, we woke up one morning to find that snow had fallen, and it briefly gave us a magical source of light under a leaden sky. This time the bare, snow-covered fields were a perfect foreground for our shots of the old parish church of St Peter and St Paul, where the choir was beginning to sing 'In the bleak mid-winter'.

When Christina Rossetti wrote her poem sometime after 1850, she had no idea that it would be set to music or sung as a carol. A devout high Anglican, Christina was a very pious and intense person, even by Victorian standards. She had at least one unhappy love affair and was never to marry. Her great love was an artist, James Collinson, a member of the Pre-Raphaelite Brotherhood

Christina Rossetti, by Dante Gabriel Rossetti (1866)

– a group of artists who aspired to great moral seriousness. But their engagement was broken off in 1850 when he joined the Roman Catholic Church. Much of her later poetry is pervaded by a sense of melancholy and the recurrent themes of unhappy or frustrated love.

Christina turned more and more to her devotion to God. Her brother, the artist Dante Gabriel Rossetti, conveyed her quality of mystical yearning when he asked her to sit for his portrait of the Virgin Mary.

A friend of her brother, the painter William Holman Hunt, also persuaded her to model for *The Light of the World*, a famous painting which depicts Jesus, outside on a dark, winter night, lantern in hand, knocking at a door. The painting can be seen today in St Paul's Cathedral in London, and Christina's complexion provided the model for the skin tones of Christ. Holman Hunt described Christina as 'exactly the pure and docile-hearted damsel that her brother portrayed God's Virgin to be'.

But Christina Rossetti was to show herself to be much more than merely an obedient, artists' model. In her yearning for love and fulfilment she turned to writing, and perhaps this yearning was never more intensely expressed than in what today is the nation's favourite carol, the last verse of which can move grown men and women to tears.

Whether standing in our overcoats in a cold, dim church, or listening to the soaring sound of a cathedral choir, 'In the bleak mid-winter' springs a surprise on us and touches our hearts just when we are thinking of settling down to traditional Christmas indulgence and all the trimmings. The carol expresses the wonder of how, in the most unlikely circumstances – in a desolate, out-of-the-way corner when life itself would hardly seem possible – God comes to us as a frail baby. Watched over by the angels, the simple animals are the only earthly witnesses to the birth, sheltering Joseph and Mary and warming the child in the manger with their breath. Then come the shepherds and the wise men. A sublimely happy Mary kisses the child, and suddenly the writer strips off all the trappings of the world of the artist's model and the languid, mannered sophistication of Victorian painters, and asks what she has to give in response to this event that changes the world for ever: 'What can I give him, poor as I am?'

Alison Elliot, first woman and first lay person to be moderator of the General Assembly of the Church of Scotland, and holder of a hugely responsible job, had no hesitation in nominating this as her favourite carol. Just after it had been sung at a special carol service for the great and the good of Edinburgh in 2004, she told me, 'I was in tears throughout the last verse. I always am.' So I was not surprised when, a few days later, Alison Elliot became the first church leader from Britain to change her busy planned schedule to travel instead to the devastated country of Sri Lanka to show solidarity with the faith communities as they struggled to cope with the unimaginable horror of the tsunami. She believed that, for anyone who sings the last two lines of the carol, there could be no choice.

The other ingredient that makes this carol so popular is the tune. There are in fact two well-loved tunes. The oldest is *Cranham* by Gustav Holst. Included 100 years ago in *The English Hymnal*, it is the one usually sung by congregations. But in 1911 a young London organist, Harold Darke, wrote the tune that choristers prefer and, strangely enough, this is the only tune to have been asked for by name over and over again on the voting forms for the nation's favourite carol. 'Make sure it is the DARKE tune!' many voters have written in block capitals. This has made me notice, really for the first time, how perfectly this tune and the words complement each other.

Not long after writing the tune, Harold Darke started a special choir at St Michael's, Cornhill, where he was the organist for 50 years. Many London office workers will remember the wonderful, calm oasis in the day provided by his lunch-time organ recitals. Even in the middle of the London Blitz during the Second World War, Harold Darke rehearsed and conducted impromptu

The Light of the World by William Holman Hunt (1853)

In the bleak mid-winter
frosty wind made moan,
earth stood hard as iron,
water like a stone;
snow had fallen, snow on snow,
snow on snow,
in the bleak mid-winter,
long ago.

Our God, heaven cannot hold him,
nor earth sustain;
heaven and earth shall flee away
when he comes to reign:
in the bleak mid-winter
a stable-place sufficed
the Lord God Almighty,
Jesus Christ.

Enough for him, whom cherubim
worship night and day,
a breastful of milk,
and a mangerful of hay;
enough for him, whom angels
fall down before,
the ox and ass and camel
which adore.

Angels and archangels
may have gathered there,
cherubim and seraphim
thronged the air;
but his mother only,
in her maiden bliss,
worshipped the Belovèd
with a kiss.

What can I give him,
poor as I am?
If I were a shepherd,
I would bring a lamb;
if I were a wise man,
I would do my part;
yet what I can I give him –
give my heart.

performances of Handel's *Messiah* for
anyone who wanted to come and sing.
Listening recently to his communion
setting in the Sunday service in St Mary's
Cathedral in Edinburgh, I suddenly
recognised a familiar pattern of notes. As
they sang the 'Benedictus', 'Blessed is he
who comes in the Name of the Lord', barely
disguised in the choir's part was an echo of
'In the bleak mid-winter'.

How utterly astonished Christina
Rossetti would have been to know how
many of us are still being drawn to a deeper
understanding of Christmas by her poem.

It came upon the midnight clear

6

Preparing to film *Songs of Praise* begins with the camera director seeking the quietest corner that he or she can find to hide in. For one day at least, they must forget everything and everyone else. For the 30 years that I was a director, the routine was always the same: solitary confinement armed with a mug of tea and a hymn book. I would sit and stare into space for hours – at least that is what it would look like to anyone unlucky enough to discover my hiding place. The tea would become more and more stewed, but it was strangely comforting as I worked to envisage in my mind's eye what every second of the finished TV programme would look like on the screen. The average viewer is rightly unaware that every single picture on their screens has been visualised and written down in the form of a script before the cameras have even arrived at the church or cathedral where the hymns are sung. If the audience enjoys seeing a Christmas carol on *Songs of Praise*, it means the director has done their job properly.

One director decided that he could make the whole programme up as he went along – it would look more spontaneous that way. For a very long evening, the cameras rushed up and down, banging into each other and only just avoiding the singers. They all kept focusing on the same pretty girl (as mentioned earlier, the director was male!), and it was fortunate that the singers, the musicians and the vicar were prepared to come back the next night, by which time a haggard, red-eyed, crest-fallen director had produced a script, like everyone else.

I was thinking about the 'invisible works' behind *Songs of Praise* after watching the 2004 Christmas programme from Ely Cathedral. For the first time, I was moved by a carol that I had never before given much thought to: Edmund Sears's 'It came upon the midnight clear'. 'I wonder if it will make the short list?' said Jonathan Edwards, the presenter, before it was sung that night. It turned out to be one of the nation's top twenty, but I wonder how many viewers were like me and voted for this carol mainly because of the way it was shown that night.

I have discovered that a great many of the best-known carols that we all join in with today were written during a 25-year period beginning around 1845, when Queen Victoria was on the throne of the British Empire. Travel was no longer the preserve of the very rich and the Industrial Revolution was spreading around the world. Yet slavery was still a source of ill-gotten gain and, in North America, black people as a whole lived in great poverty.

Edmund Sears wrote 'It came upon the midnight clear' in 1846, when America was heading towards a civil war which was to divide north from south and brother from brother. Sears was living in the small town of Wayland in Massachusetts where he was a pastor and edited a religious magazine. His first hymn, written while he was still a student, was called 'Calm on the listening ear of night'. I am unable to find the words, but it does sound from the title that it could have been an earlier version or a prelude to 'It came upon the midnight clear'.

The carol depicts the glorious moment when angels appeared at Bethlehem, and asks us to help spread their message of peace and goodwill in our own lives. We cannot be mere bystanders marvelling at the scene over which the angels hover, for now we are all involved.

Even in his rural corner of America, Edmund Sears must have known that cruelty and violence were never far beneath the surface. His carol somehow breaks out of its Victorian frame and describes a still all-too-recognisable world. When the congregation in the nave of Ely Cathedral sang, 'Yet with the woes of sin and strife the world has suffered long,' they were echoing what every TV news bulletin that night in 2004 was showing us, not only from Israel/Palestine, which is still the Holy Land, but also from Iraq and America and on our own doorsteps.

Paul Trepte, organist of Ely Cathedral, who rehearsed and conducted the carols, began by asking each singer to think about

the meaning of the words before they sang even a note of music. David Kremer, one of the most experienced and meticulous directors of *Songs of Praise*, had clearly been doing the same thing during his own time of preparation, 'staring into space' and envisioning the shots in his mind's eye before he set out for Ely.

David alternated huge, wide-angle shots showing the beauty of the ancient cathedral and its unique painted roof, with quite intimate shots of the singers gathered below in the nave. Each person was holding a candle that lit up their face – young innocence side by side with the old and care-worn. The gentle lighting conveyed so much more character than was possible in the early days of *Songs of Praise*,

when huge lamps simply floodlit everyone.

The flat fen country around Ely is home to many British and American airbases, as a war memorial in the cathedral shows. As the choir began singing verse 3 –

Yet with the woes of sin and strife,
the world has suffered long,

– which resonated with the day's news, the camera shots switched between different men and women in the congregation, so that they seemed to be having a conversation. How many, I wondered as I watched them, had sons or daughters on duty in Iraq?

The young generation, from the King's School in the city, responded:

It came upon the midnight clear,
that glorious song of old,
from angels bending near the earth
to touch their harps of gold:
'Peace on the earth, good-will to men,
from heaven's all-gracious King';
the world in solemn stillness lay
to hear the angels sing.

Still through the cloven skies they come,
with peaceful wings unfurled;
and still their heavenly music floats
o'er all the weary world:
above its sad and lowly plains
they bend on hovering wing;
and ever o'er its Babel sounds
the blessed angels sing.

Yet with the woes of sin and strife
the world has suffered long;
beneath the angel-strain have rolled
two thousand years of wrong;
and man, at war with man, hears not
the love-song which they bring:
O hush the noise, ye men of strife,
and hear the angels sing.

For lo! the days are hastening on,
by prophet bards foretold,
when with the ever-circling years
comes round the age of gold;
when peace shall over all the earth
its ancient splendours fling,
and all the world give back the song
which now the angels sing.

O hush the noise, ye men of strife,
and hear the angels sing.

As a camera revealed the ranks of carved and painted angels high above our heads, it suddenly became a moment of intense prayerfulness.

'Yes,' the Victorian author might have said if he could have been in Ely that night. 'That's what I hoped might happen.'

At Christmas 2005, *Songs of Praise* cameras will be in Lincoln Cathedral. Each carol, looked at with as much care, will give us more images to deepen our understanding of what Paul Trepte at Ely called 'the greatest story ever told'.

Perhaps some of the people who took part in the last Christmas *Songs of Praise*

from the great Minster Church some years ago, high on the hill above Lincoln, will be among the singers once again. *Songs of Praise* took part in a long-running tradition, in which listeners to BBC Radio Lincoln come together for a special carol service at the cathedral; but the director, Chris Mann, introduced a startling new feature. Chris, one of *Songs of Praise*'s most imaginative and flamboyant directors, wasn't nicknamed Cecil B. de Mann for nothing. I hope everyone who remembers Chris's often almost uncontrollable acts of creativity, thought up as he prepared his scripts at his kitchen table, has long forgiven him for the extraordinary demands he used to make.

This time, while the carol singers were congregating in a Christmas street-market in Lincoln, Chris sent his production assistant, Sue, hundreds of feet up to the very top of one of the cathedral towers so that at the appropriate moment a real live angel would suddenly be revealed. Waiting in the dark on top of a high tower on a freezing cold December night, the 'angel', clad in about six layers of duffel coat under her white angelic costume and wings, was suddenly lit up by powerful lights – and helped to create a moment of pure TV magic for us all. She may still be thawing out.

Joy to the world
<u>18</u>

It is a brave person who tries to stand still when commuters are streaming across the concourse at London's Victoria Station during the rush hour. As Christmas Eve approaches, members of the Salvation Army band take up the challenge. Near the station Christmas tree the euphonium player, with a frame as formidable as his instrument, has his feet planted firmly apart to establish his territory. His cheerful face, clearly created for smiling, is coaxing coins and notes out of the pockets of stressed and weary travellers even before he joins his colleagues to 'oohmpah' his way through 'Joy to the world'.

Isaac Watts

Arriving at Victoria as Handel's tune 'Antioch' resonates under the cathedral-like acoustic of the station's high glass roof, I am irresistibly drawn towards them. As I stop to watch the small band of young and old musicians who, unlike the barging commuters, all seem so at ease with each other, I nearly get flattened. I battle on and out of the station, but when I come back two hours later, there they are, still gathered by the Christmas tree, still smiling, and still playing 'Joy to the world'.

In order to find the origins of 'Joy to the world' we must take a long journey almost 300 years back through time. Isaac Watts, preacher and minister of the gospel, was born in Southampton in 1674. His family had suffered for their faith: his father was twice imprisoned as a dissenter. Isaac himself had been frail and sickly for years when he wrote his carol in 1719.

For more than 50 years after the end of the Civil War, England had alternated between Catholic and Protestant monarchs and parliaments. In the early years of the eighteenth century the mood in the country was still jittery; they were strange, rumour-filled days. Newspapers had just begun to spread in England, and with them came rumours of wars and foreign invaders. The weather was peculiar too. There was the hardest frost for years on Christmas Day 1709: the Thames froze over and the river fell to such a low level that people could walk under the arches of London Bridge. After

Joy to the world, the Lord has come!
Let earth receive her King;
let every heart prepare him room,
and heaven and nature sing.

Joy to the earth, the Saviour reigns!
Your sweetest songs employ;
while fields and streams and hills and
   plains
repeat the sounding joy.

He rules the world with truth and grace,
and makes the nations prove
the glories of his righteousness,
the wonders of his love.

that came a plague of flies of almost biblical proportions. The infamous South Sea Company was expanding in the City of London, and investors were enthusiastically parting with their money in increasingly unlikely speculations, such as a company that built a 'flying machine' and another that made a 'perpetual motion machine'.

There was a newspaper report that 'loose, idle and disorderly people' on the streets at the weekends stopped the traffic and assaulted travellers – a scenario only too familiar in the news today. Christians were also at risk, as mobs attacked and destroyed the Meeting Houses where austere, Bible-believing dissenters who had left the established church met.

The rumours bordered on the absurd when a party of American Indians appeared in London, claiming that they had been told that 'the Saviour of the World' had been born in France and crucified in England.

At Christmas 1719, as Isaac Watts completed the words for 'Joy to the world', the South Sea bubble was about to burst, leaving thousands ruined. In this unstable and nervy world, the words of Isaac Watts's carol introduced a new idea to the hymnody of the time. He drew on a psalm from the Old Testament, a method prescribed by the established church in its hymn-writing; but then, by adding a verse from Paul's letter to the Romans, he quoted the New Testament – which had never been done before. Verses from Psalm 98, in which creation celebrates the kingship of God, and a verse from Genesis about the earth being cursed as a result of Adam's disobedience in the Garden of Eden, are completed by a verse from the apostle Paul about the love offered to humankind through the life, death and resurrection of the baby born in Bethlehem. The famous Handel tune to which the carol is sung is called 'Antioch', a place also associated with Paul – the site of the earliest known Christian community, where the word 'Christian' was first used.

Watts's carol, as with his better known hymns like 'O God, our help in ages past' and, greatest of all, 'When I survey the wondrous cross', offered joy, hope and meaning to an anxious world.

Isaac Watts's words, both then and now, appeal to Christians who are breaking new ground. Although today 'Joy to the world' is a favourite component of the traditional carol 'medley' performed by Salvation Army bands, such as Paul Leddington Wright's new arrangement which began the 2004 *Songs of Praise* 'Christmas Big Sing' in the Royal Albert Hall, it also resonates perfectly

with the message at the heart of the fast-growing Hillsong Church. Founded in 1983 with just 45 members, there are now more than 17,000 people 'doing church', as they call it, every Sunday in Australia, Russia and London.

Like the apostle Paul, the Hillsong Church is always on the move: they do not even have their own church buildings, and the London branch currently hires a big cinema in London's West End for three services, each of which draws a capacity crowd. For *Songs of Praise* on Advent Sunday they gathered in the Mermaid Theatre in the City of London.

This was a programme fit to dispel tea-time slumbers in the television audience. Supported by an eight-ton state-of-the-art sound and lighting system and their own rock band, almost 400 Hillsong members rocked through the night to share their faith. When

'Joy to the world' was sung, everyone began rhythmically waving their arms and you could see that, given more space, they would all have been dancing. It is a young church. Rock music artists and actors rub shoulders with city bankers, accountants and stock-market gurus. Ethically motivated by their faith, and far more astute than the entrepreneurs creating the South Sea bubble in Isaac Watts's day, Hillsong members sign up to giving their money and their time 'until it hurts'.

Which brings me back to those other musicians, blowing and beating out Isaac Watts's carol at Victoria Station, who care for all in need and stand still in the middle of a rushing, nervy, anxiety-laden crowd to bring joy to the world.

Long time ago in Bethlehem
(Mary's boy child)
11

Jestie Hairston was born in North Carolina in 1902. He was a distinguished singer, composer and actor, and lived to a grand old age, dying in January 2000. If you are a classic American TV and radio buff, you will know him from the series *Amos and Andy*, and perhaps as Deacon Forbes from the show *Amen*.

I don't know a lot about American TV comedy, but I was fortunate enough to have once been on the set of *The Beverley Hillbillies* when Phil Silvers, who played Sergeant Bilko, was making a guest appearance, and I think Hairston belonged to the same generation of natural comedians. I can imagine he lived up to the nickname given to him by his first teacher – 'Jester'. Comedy, as all who loved the late Dame Thora Hird know, is not just a fine art but a God-given talent, and *Amen* seems to have been as popular as Dame Thora's own series *Hallelujah*.

Jester came from humble origins. Although he was fortunate enough to be able to go to university, like many students today he had to earn his living in the holidays.

While working in the docks in Boston, he taught his fellow workers to sing. In the Depression years of the 1930s he was lucky enough to find his first job as a music teacher, and at the same time he became a member of the famous black singing group of the day, the Hall Johnson Choir. In 1951 he appeared in a weekly radio series starring Humphrey Bogart, which went on for 78 episodes. Jester played the part of King Moses, a calypso singer, and his songs provided musical bridges in each episode. For 30 years he also arranged film music, including the scores of *Gunfight at the OK*

Hall Johnson conducting his Hall Johnson Negro Choir in the 1920s

Corral and *The Guns of Navarone.*

What matters to us however in our search for the nation's favourite carol, is that Jester Hairston wrote and arranged more than 300 spirituals, and in particular the words and tune of 'Long time ago in Bethlehem'. I first got to know this carol as 'Mary's boy child' through hearing it sung by Harry Belafonte on *Housewives' Choice* on the old BBC *Light Programme* (*everybody* listened to it in those days). It must have been one of only a few carols to feature in the old 'hit parade', and I still remember the sound of Harry Belafonte's familiar relaxed voice and the calypso rhythm whenever it is sung in church.

'Mary's boy child' has a chorus that in utterly simple words sums up the good news of the gospel entirely. It expresses the Christmas message so beautifully, but the words also come into my head all through the year, whenever I find myself getting wound up in theological knots:

Trumpets sound and angels sing,
listen to what they say,
that we may live for evermore,
because of Christmas Day.

There's another song from the era of *Housewives' Choice* that I have been unable to get out of my head recently. The chorus goes:

Enjoy yourself, enjoy yourself,
it's later than you think.

It makes me vaguely uneasy, and I think that means I still have a lot of catching up to do.

Harry Belafonte in 1954 with his daughter, Adrienne

Twenty-five years ago I visited the state of North Carolina, where Jester was born, to meet the world-famous evangelist, Dr Billy Graham. I don't know if the two men ever met, but I think they would have had a lot in common. In the foothills of the Blue Ridge Mountains we sat in the garden of Dr Graham's unpretentious home, surrounded by the beauties of creation, and for the first time I came to appreciate Dr Graham's own simple language and direct appeal. No longer the 'hell-fire and damnation' preacher of old news film, but a quiet and thoughtful man of God, Dr Graham has lived a long and fulfilled life which has been of benefit to others. Jester Hairston's life of faith was also long and well spent – he was

Long time ago in Bethlehem,
so the Holy Bible say;
Mary's boy child Jesus Christ
was born on Christmas Day.

Hark now hear the angels sing,
a new king born today,
and we will live forever more,
because of Christmas Day.

Trumpets sound and angels sing,
listen to what they say,
that we may live for evermore,
because of Christmas Day.

Now Joseph and his wife Mary,
come to Bethlehem that night,
she have no place to bear her child,
not a single room was in sight.

By and by they find a little nook,
in a stable all forlorn,
and in a manger cold and dark,
Mary's little boy was born.

still conducting choirs into his 90s – and, like Dr Graham, he always lived in the Advent hope of the second coming of Christ.

Blue Ridge Mountains, North Carolina

O come, all ye faithful

5

An attempt to get to the bottom of the story of one of our best-known carols, sung at Christmas time all around the world, might cause even a detective of the calibre of Agatha Christie's Hercule Poirot to admit defeat. The familiar words and tune emerge from a misty past. On its way into the current *Songs of Praise* hymn book, people have claimed that the tune is English, or French, or German, or Portuguese in origin.

Prince Charles Eduard Stewart by Louis Gabriel Blanchet

The words have been suspected of containing a secret code that identifies the singer with the Jacobite Cause that led both to the most recent battles fought on British soil and then eventually to the defeat of the Young Pretender, Bonnie Prince Charlie, in 1746. So beware confusion and conjecture as we try to unravel the mystery.

The first suspect we encounter when tracing the author of the tune is John Reading, organist of Winchester College, who died in 1692. He has as his witness Vincent Novello, the famous nineteenth-century organist, who said that Reading had set the tune to a metrical version of Psalm 106. So in 1906 the English composer Ralph Vaughan Williams, working with the priest Percy Dearmer to edit the *English Hymnal*, may well have tried to sing these metrical words to the carol tune. If one uses the Church of Scotland's metrical version of the psalm, 'Give praise and thanks unto the Lord, for bountiful is he', it is just possible – I've tried it. But sung to the older, late seventeenth-century English version of Psalm 106 by Tate and Brady, 'O render thanks to God above, the fountain of eternal love', the result is ridiculous. The editors of the *English Hymnal* looked through all of Novello's papers and could find nothing else to back up his claim. Case dismissed.

In a further complication to the story, in around 1785 the Duke of Leeds happened to hear the tune at the Portuguese Chapel in London, where Novello was the organist, and so concluded that it had come originally from Portugal. For years after it was referred to as 'the Portuguese Hymn'.

A more likely suspect is John Wade, who at some time between 1740 and 1744 set the tune to 'Adeste Fideles', the Latin words of which are still sung by Roman Catholics across the world. Wade was a student at that time, working as a music copier at Douai Abbey in France. It is possible that he took the words, 'Adeste Fideles' – which he may have written himself or may have heard sung in plainchant by the monks – and set them to a tune from a comic-opera, *Acajou*, which was being performed in Paris at the time.

The question arises: why was Wade still in Douai – when on 15 March 1744 France declared war on England? Could he have been a Jacobite spy? A month earlier Charles, the Stewart Pretender, had been on the brink of invading England, and only a storm had stopped his army of 15,000 men from sailing. In May 1745 the *London Magazine* published a letter from an English army officer, who was actually being held hostage in Douai because one of the French enemy, the Maréchal de Bellisle, had been captured and taken to the Tower of London. So here is the tenuous but exotic source of the idea that it had been written as a rallying call for the Pretender's cause – 'O come, all ye faithful'.

By 1751 John Wade was at Stoneyhurst College in Lancashire, once again working for Catholic families and priests, and still

O come, all ye faithful,
joyful and triumphant,
O come ye, O come ye to Bethlehem:
come and behold him
born the King of angels:

O come, let us adore him,
O come, let us adore him,
O come, let us adore him,
Christ the Lord!

God of God,
Light of light,
lo, he abhors not the virgin's womb;
very God,
begotten, not created:

See how the shepherds,
summoned to his cradle,
leaving their flocks, draw nigh with lowly fear;
we too will thither
bend our joyful footsteps:

Lo, star-led chieftains,
magi, Christ adoring,
offer him incense, gold and myrrh;
we to the Christ-child
bring our hearts' oblations:

Sing, choirs of angels,
sing in exultation,
sing, all ye citizens of heaven above,
'Glory to God
in the highest':

Yea, Lord, we greet thee,
born this happy morning,
Jesu, to thee be glory given;
Word of the Father,
now in flesh appearing:

copying music. There he published 'Adeste Fideles' as his own work, but the tune used then would not have sounded familiar to our ears because it was set in triple time, in the style of a waltz rather than a solemn processional. However, John Wade is still the most likely person to have written the tune that we all now know and love.

Since 'Adeste Fideles' was first published, there have been at least 38 different translations into English, including the one we know best, written by Frederick Oakeley, the nineteenth-century Anglican vicar of All Saints', Margaret Street in London, who along with John Henry Newman was later to become a Roman Catholic. His original translation began rather less compellingly: 'Ye faithful, approach ye, joyfully triumphant'.

John Henry Newman's thoughts about writing hymns, quoted by the editors in the preface to the 1925 *Hymn Book* created for the University of Oxford, show why the rich but unsentimental verses of 'O come, all ye faithful', translated by his friend Frederick Oakeley, still mean so much:

Prune thou thy words, the thoughts control
That o'er thee swell and throng;
They will condense within thy soul
And change to purpose strong.

At the end of these rather fruitless enquiries, 'O come, all ye faithful' is, as the votes have revealed, still one of the nation's favourite carols. It is also one of the best known, and when the BBC cameras were in Westminster Cathedral on Christmas Eve 2001, the famous cathedral choir led Cardinal Cormac Murphy O'Connor out of

the darkness of the nave into the dramatically lit basilica singing 'Adeste Fideles' – and everybody seemed to know the words by heart.

While each verse sung in carol services in the weeks before Christmas draws us into the company of shepherds and wise men at the manger at Bethlehem, the final

verse should be, and usually is, reserved for singing on Christmas morning. In St Mary's Episcopal Cathedral in Edinburgh, the climax of the Christmas Day communion comes as the bishop raises the consecrated bread and wine from the altar, and everyone remains kneeling to sing, 'Yea, Lord, we greet thee, born this happy morning.'

It is a moment when all distractions about spies and codes and light opera and metrical psalms are forgotten, and the still-anonymous author points us to the event at the heart of Christmas. Both simple and yet beyond comprehension, this is the story that counts.

The Adoration of the Kings by Hans Memling (fifteenth century)

O holy night
4

This carol was described as having the 'X factor' when it emerged top of the poll of 'Favourite Carols' on one radio station in the Christmas of 2004. You might even call it the 'star' factor because of the great variety of famous voices who have recorded it – from popular artists like Perry Como, Mahalia Jackson, Nat King Cole, G4 and Destiny's Child, to the classical voices of Luciano Pavarotti and sopranos Joan Sutherland and Leontyne Price (singing with the world-famous Vienna Philharmonic Orchestra conducted by the legendary Herbert von Karijan). To say nothing of all the many great cathedral choirs and choral societies all over the world that include it every year in their repertoire.

But a recent performance by the Welsh mezzo-soprano Kathryn Jenkins who, like celebrity soloists Aled Jones and Hayley Westenra, sings on *Songs of Praise*, had the most surprising result of all. As she sang 'O holy night' in front of a live audience, her pure intonation and impeccably pitched top note literally shattered a glass chandelier just above her head. The young singer's performance not only proved a scientific experiment that every school-boy yearns to demonstrate, but revealed cool professionalism as she sang on, unmoved.

France is not a country with a strong tradition of carol singing, but in 1847, Placide Clappeau, an amateur poet and the mayor of a little town near Avignon called Roquemaure, wrote a Christmas poem at the request of his local parish priest. The mayor of even the smallest town or village in France is always an immensely important person and especially so, I suspect, in the case of Monsieur Clappeau, who was also the local wine merchant. While the hard-working mayor or provost of a town in Britain may not be instantly recognised, every mayor in France is greatly respected and sets the tone for the community. Mayor Clappeau took his poem to Paris, to a friend of a friend – the famous composer of *Giselle*, Charles Adolphe Adam – who wrote a tune for the poem in a few days. The song received its première at the midnight mass in Roquemaure on Christmas Eve 1847. It was an instant success.

What seems incredible today is that this beautiful song was soon to be attacked by churchmen in Clappeau's native France. The criticism was based not on the intrinsic merits of the song but on the reputations of both lyricist and composer. Late in his life Clappeau had become a freethinker, adopting some of the 'extreme' political and social views of his era – such as opposition to inequality, slavery and injustice of all kinds.

Moreover Adam, the composer, was Jewish. These beliefs were deemed incompatible with the composition of a Christian religious song.

Fortunately more rational perspectives prevailed. By 1855 the carol had been published in London and has now been translated into many languages. The best-known English translation is by an American, John Sullivan Dwight, a Unitarian minister who was also a music critic and journalist.

'O holy night' is a perfect Christmas song for the soloist brave enough to stand alone and sing all three verses. They describe the starlit night of nights when the birth of a Saviour brings hope and a new dawn to a sad and pining earth. Then, led by the light of a star, the wise men from the Orient arrive to find the King of kings in a lowly manger. The last verse talks of how his gospel of peace will break our chains of slavery and oppression. The rest of us croakers take up the choruses, encouraging each other to worship the infant Jesus at the heart of this scene.

But let me award the brightest 'star' to singer and presenter of *Songs of Praise*, Aled Jones, for his two recordings, first as boy and then as man, which have been brought together as one by the miracle of modern technology. When the brilliant young treble from Bangor Cathedral Choir sang the song on *Songs of Praise* in 1984, little could he have imagined that twenty years later his performance would become one half of a duet with his grown-up self.

The director of Libera, the boys' choir from South London that features regularly on *Songs of Praise* and has even appeared on *Top of the Pops*, Robert Prizeman is also an invisible force at recordings. He is the man who often, to the amusement of the congregation, telephones the conductor in the pulpit when *Songs of Praise* is being rehearsed. As the singers wait in suspense

to hear whether a hymn must be sung for a second, or tenth, time, Robert is delivering his verdict down the telephone from the control vehicle where he listens. If you aren't singing with enough enthusiasm, or he can't make out the words, beware – Robert will make you do it again.

For the famous duet recording, arranged by Prizeman, the light, tenor voice of the grown-up Aled has blended perfectly with his younger treble tones, and both voices unite with great sensitivity. It sounds so effortless but it must have been hard to do. There are all sorts of technical devices that can bring voices together, but as a former sound technician I am fairly certain that this was recorded 'in a oner' – in one go, without sound edits.

There is, however, all the difference in the world between enjoying listening to a beautifully produced CD by Aled, or even watching him on television, and singing in your own local church at Christmas. As much as I will never forget Aled's version, I shall also not forget a local group, members of St Mary's Roman Catholic Church, and their performance in our Midlothian village. For ten years the local community has gathered for a Christmas carol service in the fifteenth-century Crichton Collegiate Kirk. In this time all the favourite and familiar carols have been sung, as well as played by hand-bell ringers and even a quartet of young bassoon players. Recently, reflecting hopes for Christian unity, we have been joined – in what for centuries has been very much a Presbyterian atmosphere – by our Roman Catholic neighbours.

'Oh, I don't think that we can offer you much,' was the choir director Moira's response when I first asked if they would come along and sing some solo and choir items. How glad I am that I took no notice and persuaded them to come anyway.

The choir swelled our congregation, and there was no doubt that there had been a great deal of preparation. When the moment came for 'O holy night', one of the singers, Ian, who is somewhat older than Aled, gently sang the first verse and then the little choir joined in the chorus. By the second and third verses, everyone was singing the chorus and some people were in tears. Under the medieval vaulted stone roof, where more than 500 years ago priests and singing boys sang the Christmas mass, Ian brought us old Protestants the 'thrill of hope, the weary world rejoices'.

As we went out into the dark night, Advent had become Christmas and we had all received our first Christmas present.

O holy night, the stars are brightly shining;
it is the night of the dear Saviour's birth!
Long lay the world in sin and error pining,
till He appeared and the soul felt its worth.
A thrill of hope, the weary world rejoices,
for yonder breaks a new and glorious morn.
Fall on your knees, O hear the angel voices!
O night divine, O night when Christ was born!
O night, O holy night, O night divine!

Led by the light of faith serenely beaming,
with glowing hearts by His cradle we stand.
So led by light of a star sweetly gleaming,
here came the wise men from Orient land.
The King of kings lay thus in lowly manger,
in all our trials born to be our Friend!
He knows our need – to our weakness is no stranger.
Behold your King; before Him lowly bend!
Behold your King; before Him lowly bend!

Truly He taught us to love one another;
His law is love and His Gospel is peace.
Chains shall He break for the slave is our brother
and in His Name all oppression shall cease.
Sweet hymns of joy in grateful chorus raise we,
let all within us praise His holy Name!
Christ is the Lord! O praise His name forever!
His pow'r and glory evermore proclaim!
His pow'r and glory evermore proclaim!

O little town of Bethlehem

7

I have never been to Bethlehem, and with the tragic conflict currently making life in the little town such a struggle, many of us will only ever see this holy place on the TV news. But until recently it had been a popular place of pilgrimage for nearly 2,000 years.

On Christmas Eve in 1865, a young American rode on horseback across Palestine to Bethlehem. Phillips Brooks had taken a year out from running his parish in Philadelphia and this was to be the final, and most moving, destination of his pilgrimage. The American went to the Church of the Nativity in Manger Square in Bethlehem, where he attended the five-hour-long service to celebrate Christmas Eve at the very place where Christ was born.

Brooks was a huge man given to voluble speech; it was said that he preached 'with the impetuosity of a mountain torrent – two hundred and fifty words a minute – too fast for anyone to take down'. The scenes he saw in the Holy Land that Christmas must have given him a new sensitivity and delicacy, which were expressed as he wrote the five simple verses of his hymn. He wrote in his diary:

Before dark, we rode to the field where they say the shepherds saw the Angel. It is a fenced piece of ground with a cave in it… Somewhere in those fields we rode through, the shepherds must have been… As we passed, some shepherds were still 'keeping watch over their flocks'.

At the heart of Phillips Brooks's hymn, which evokes the image of an ordinary little town very like our own little towns and villages, is the verse beginning 'How silently, how silently, the wondrous gift is given…'. Where there is a choir, they will often sing this alone, allowing the rest of us to meditate, but even slightly tipsy congregations at a busy midnight mass usually manage to sing this verse as gently and thoughtfully as it deserves. The theme of silence not only conveys the awe we feel as 'the wondrous gift is given', but it is a reminder of the medieval belief that the virgin birth was marked by complete silence.

Silence and light. Medieval paintings depicting the nativity scene show the face of Jesus literally lighting up the darkened stable, 'the everlasting light' that Brooks writes of in the opening verse; and, standing in a darkened church, I always notice at this point how the choristers' faces glow in the candlelight.

Once, and I think only once, my late father sang in the choir for the carol service in his

Cambridge College, Magdalene. After he had died I found his prayer book, in which were typed the words of the hymn. At verse 3, there were a series of ruled lines and the numbers 1 and 2, which baffled me because it looked exactly like a director's camera script for *Songs of Praise*. I stared at it for ages. Certainly my father had been in places where John Logie Baird had been, and at the time he was inventing TV. Could he – who at first dividing the brilliantly lit streets of West Berlin from the dark, gloomy roads of the communist East. The whole city felt claustrophobic, and although there were many prayers for peace and reconciliation, we could not see any hope of the astonishing events that were to come ten years later when the separated citizens of Berlin tore down the wall that divided them, without bloodshed.

had so disapproved of my own chosen career – possibly have been trying to write a proto-television script? In the end a kindly organist pointed out the obvious: the singers had been split into two parts. 'Get a life!' he might have added.

Songs of Praise has been broadcast from Israel/Palestine; but my own most vivid memory of the hymn is of a recording I made in another divided city. In 1978, I directed the Christmas programme from Berlin. The hideous concrete wall was still in place,

On the day of our recording, armed guards watched closely as we looked at one piece of the wall where the word 'Jesus' stood out among the graffiti, near to where people were still being shot dead as they tried to escape to the West. We heard stories of the war, and of the aftermath of the war. In the 'Blue Church', the British, French and American communities that made up the NATO defence forces, together with even a few Russians, sang the hymn as snow fell outside on the famous *Kaiserwilhelmstrasse*.

As I have been writing about the nation's favourite carols, friends have asked how I can still sing a hymn that evokes peace and light when the reality for Jews and Muslims – as well as Christians – living in Israel/Palestine is so different. An answer of sorts has come from the singer Martin John Nicholls, who was commissioned by Christian Aid to visit all the communities in and around a broken and deserted Bethlehem that are still working for peace and justice in the Middle East. Martin found that, unnoticed behind the news headlines, there are many thousands of people who refuse to turn to violence.

As he listened to their stories, he decided that he wanted to write a new carol, new words and new music, about Bethlehem. He calls it 'Broken town'. It begins 'Broken town of Bethlehem your people long for peace.' Here is his third verse:

Holy streets of Bethlehem
deserted and destroyed.
The frightened faces fill the sacred places
pilgrims once enjoyed.
Yet in the midst of darkness
a hopeful beacon shines:
The future lies in humble sacrifice
and not in guns and mines.
and not in guns and mines.

An Israeli tank faces the Church of the Nativity, Manger Square, Bethlehem, May 2002

Martin tells me that, thanks to the wonders of e-mail, his new carol is now sung around the world, but in particular at Christmas time in Bethlehem.

I am probably an old stick-in-the-mud and prefer to sing Phillips Brooks's words to Ralph Vaughan Williams's tune 'Forest Green', which originated no closer to Bethlehem than Sussex. Even so, I always think of the brave people of Bethlehem whose stories have enabled Martin John Nicholls to write his carol. Just as the world was not ready for the event that changed history in Bethlehem 2,000 years ago, and just as I did not dream of the end of the Cold War while directing *Songs of Praise* in 1978, I remember that Emmanuel, the final word of both the old hymn and the new carol, means 'God with us'.

O little town of Bethlehem,
how still we see thee lie!
Above thy deep and dreamless sleep
the silent stars go by.
Yet in thy dark streets shineth
the everlasting light;
the hopes and fears of all the years
are met in thee tonight.

O morning stars, together
proclaim the holy birth
and praises sing to God the King,
and peace to all the earth.
For Christ is born of Mary;
and, gathered all above,
while mortals sleep, the angels keep
their watch of wondering love.

How silently, how silently,
the wondrous gift is given!
So God imparts to human hearts
the blessings of his heaven.
No ear may hear his coming;
but in this world of sin,
where meek souls will receive him,
still the dear Christ enters in.

Where children pure and happy
pray to the blessed child,
where misery cries out to thee,
Son of the mother mild;
where charity stands watching
and faith holds wide the door,
the dark night wakes, the glory breaks,
and Christmas comes once more.

O Holy Child of Bethlehem,
descend to us, we pray;
cast out our sin, and enter in,
be born in us today.
We hear the Christmas angels
the great glad tidings tell:
O come to us, abide with us,
our Lord Emmanuel.

On Christmas night all Christians sing

(Sussex carol)

13

On 24 May 1904, a young English organist cycled from the North Downs of Surrey into Sussex. In a cottage garden near Horsham, he listened as a folk singer sang to him. It was his first meeting with Mrs Harriet Verrall, who with her husband was still singing the old songs that her ancestors in the county had handed down for decades. One of the songs she called 'A Sussex Carol', and the young and at that time still fledgling composer, Ralph Vaughan Williams, carefully wrote down all the musical notes and words as she sang them. A century later this same carol, 'On Christmas night all Christians sing', is one of the nation's favourites.

Actually, Mrs Verrall sang him no fewer than eight songs that day, and Ralph Vaughan Williams liked her and her music so much that he went back for more. He collected a further sixteen songs from Mr and Mrs Verrall over the next year, including 'Our Captain calls', the tune of which he later used for John Bunyan's hymn, 'Who would true valour see'.

Together with his friend Cecil Sharp,

founder of the English Folk Song Society, Ralph Vaughan Williams uncovered what he described as 'the beautiful melodies hidden in the countryside'. Long before the days of broadcasting, Mrs Verrall won still more

Ralph Vaughan Williams

acclaim when she gained first prize in a local newspaper competition for the 'Best Old Sussex Song'.

Over the next few years, many other folk songs were laboriously noted down before the singers could forget them. One of the singers, a Mr Broomfield, was said to go on for hours and hours, his eyes shut tight as he sang, and he always spoke the very last line. Mr Burstow, a bell-ringer from Horsham, claimed to know over 400 songs, including some rude ones. It must have been hard work, but as a result Vaughan Williams left us not only the 'Sussex carol' but his *Fantasia on Christmas Carols*, which includes 'This is the truth sent from above', which he first heard in Herefordshire.

A few years later, along with another composer, the eccentric Australian Percy Grainger, they began using the new technology of the phonograph to record the singers. Each performance was picked up when the singer addressed a brass horn, which was connected through a vibrating diaphragm to a stylus marking a revolving wax cylinder. It became well known as the symbol of HMV Records – a little dog listening to His Master's Voice through the horn of the gramophone. To country people it must have seemed an almost magical contraption but, like all new inventions, it was a hit-and-miss device to use. It was from such apparatus in 1910 that Vaughan Williams first heard 'Come all you worthy Christians', another carol he used in his *Fantasia*.

Few people today will remember how, even before the age of the dictaphone, the office boss used to bellow down a speaking tube, recording letters onto a heated wax cylinder for the typing pool. Forty years ago, I started to collect the wax cylinders that were produced before gramophone records. Most of them are almost a hundred years old, and they are very fragile and hard to play, even on my comparatively sophisticated Edison Combination Phonograph of 1908. The machine can play back two- and four-minute recordings, and even for these the heavy clockwork spring requires a good deal of careful winding, so there is little time to enjoy 'easy' listening. At the beginning of each cylinder, the title of the music is announced together with the name of the recording company (but not, alas, the artist).

'Jack's return on Christmas Eve' is one of my favourites – a melodramatic resume of the events of one Christmas night, compressed into two minutes. We hear carol singers in the background, and then a voice intones 'Christmas Eve! And no news of our Jack. It's many a long year since he left us and it would do my old heart good to see him again.' A sharp knocking can then be heard above the hiss and crackle of the cylinder, and the speaker wonders, 'Who can that be?'

'Merry Christmas, Dad,' cries the mystery knocker. 'We've just arrived in port.'

'Why, it's our Jack!' says Dad. 'So now, lads, play us the old Christmas song.' The carollers, now joined by a brass band, burst

On Christmas night all Christians sing,
to hear the news the angels bring:
On Christmas night all Christians sing,
to hear the news the angels bring:
News of great joy, news of great mirth,
news of our merciful King's birth.

Then why should we on earth be so sad,
since our Redeemer made us glad,
then why should we on earth be so sad,
since our Redeemer made us glad,
when from our sin he set us free,
all for to gain our liberty.

When sin departs before his grace,
then life and health come in its place;
when sin departs before his grace,
then life and health come in its place;
angels and men with joy may sing,
all for to see the new-born King.

All out of darkness we have light,
which made the angels sing this night:
All out of darkness we have light,
which made the angels sing this night:
'Glory to God and peace to men,
now and for evermore. Amen.'

into a rapid verse of 'Christians, awake'...
and the fun is over.

To move from the mechanical contraptions of Vaughan Williams's pioneering days to the surround-sound technology used for today's *Songs of Praise* is to go from the ridiculous to the sublime. As Paul Trepte raised his baton to conduct a thousand singers in the nave of Ely Cathedral, I thought of Mrs Verrall's performance to an audience of one in her cottage garden a century ago, and the skill and imagination that had kept the old words and tune alive – and in the nation's top twenty favourite Christmas carols.

Once in royal David's city

8

Beloved in Christ, be it this Christmastide our care and delight to prepare ourselves to hear again the message of the Angels, and in heart and mind to go even unto Bethlehem, and see this thing which is come to pass, and the Babe lying in a manger. Let us read and mark in Holy Scripture the tales of the loving purposes of God from the first days of our disobedience unto the glorious Redemption brought us by this Holy Child: and let us make this place glad with our carols of praise.

'A BIDDING PRAYER' BY ERIC MILNER-WHITE

'You've seen the movie, now visit the set!' The huge poster outside the railway station in London last Christmas reminded me that my train journey was taking me to a place that I had seen year after year on TV, but had never before been to. The billboard showed Spiderman swooping over New York, but this had little appeal for me compared with my actual destination – the chapel of King's College, Cambridge, where I was to watch the recording of its now world-famous Festival of Nine Lessons and Carols.

At King's Cross, a crowd of Japanese tourists photographing each other in front of the fantasy 'Platform 9 ¾' – famous from the *Harry Potter* books, with its incongruous luggage trolley half-buried in the 'magic'

wall – was only a brief distraction. All my life I have wanted to be present in the university city for that moment, broadcast around the world every year, when a young treble voice from the choir is picked, seconds before going on air, to sing the first verse of 'Once in royal David's city'. This is the moment that TV or film directors would queue up to be allowed to direct; and on Christmas Eve the people of Cambridge queue from early dawn to get a seat in the chapel. Just to be there.

The story behind this annual moment of Christmas Eve magic brings together three people who never actually met: Edward Benson, first bishop of the Cornish Diocese of Truro, Eric Milner-White, First World War army chaplain who became dean at King's College, and the Irish author of 'Once in royal David's city', Mrs Cecil Frances Alexander.

At 10 pm on Christmas Eve in 1880, shortly after the foundation stone of his cathedral was laid, Bishop Benson arranged from 'ancient sources' a simple service of scripture readings and carols, held not in any sumptuous surroundings but in the wooden shed on the site – which was all that existed then. Between the singing of Christmas carols, the whole story of the 'lovingpurposes

purposes of God from the first days of our disobedience unto the glorious Redemption brought us by this Holy Child' was told with readings from the Bible by representatives of all members of the community, beginning with a young choir boy.

The bishop was hoping to discourage the unseemly, drunken revelry that had traditionally marked Christmas in England. Even without the drink, church music in those days could be a mixed blessing. Dean Hole of Rochester, a famous Victorian churchman, remembered when lusty singing was 'accompanied, preceded and followed by flute, clarinet, fiddles and bassoon… played with a good courage though not unanimous as to time or key'!

All around the world today, hundreds of services of Nine Lessons and Carols follow Bishop Benson's original 'simple' pattern; but it is thanks to Eric Milner-White, and in part to the BBC, that the service from King's College Chapel is still so popular and that its dramatic opening moment has become so famous.

MRS. ALEXANDER.
(Photograph by A. Ayton.)

Mrs Cecil Francis Alexander

In 1918, Eric Milner-White came home from the Great War to be Dean at the college where he had studied, and immediately introduced a form of Bishop Benson's service for the benefit of the citizens of Cambridge. He had a remarkable gift with words, and is best known for his 'Bidding Prayer', which always follows the singing of 'Once in royal David's city'.

In 1928, the BBC brought a smart new invention to King's College Chapel: a mobile 'outside broadcast' unit, forerunner of the gleaming, state-of-the-art control vans that now surround the ancient college gateway every Christmas. For the first broadcast, the sound engineers were able to use just six huge microphones, a fraction of what we use today. Early microphones were not sensitive, and as a former sound recordist I can easily imagine the tension in the van as they waited for the moment when the young treble voice began to sing the first lines of 'Once in royal David's city' unaccompanied. Would it even be audible to the faraway listener at their fireside?

The wonderful opening moment of this service would not have been possible without the words written by a Victorian Sunday school teacher living in rural Ireland. Mrs Cecil Frances Alexander wrote the verses to help her class of children understand part of the Apostles' Creed: 'who was conceived by the Holy Ghost and born of the Virgin Mary'. She hadn't intended it solely as a Christmas hymn, and wrote it along with other parts of the creed that she ingeniously turned into songs, which have all become just as well known and popular: 'All things bright and beautiful' and 'There is a green hill far away'.

Mrs Alexander's collection, *Hymns for Little Children*, was published in 1848 and was reprinted more than a hundred times. Its popularity increased in 1858 when 'Once

Once in royal David's city
stood a lowly cattle shed,
where a mother laid her baby
in a manger for his bed:
Mary was that mother mild,
Jesus Christ her little child.

He came down to earth from heaven,
who is God and Lord of all;
and his shelter was a stable,
and his cradle was a stall:
With the poor and mean and lowly
lived on earth our Saviour holy.

And through all his wondrous childhood
he would honour and obey,
love and watch the lowly maiden,
in whose gentle arms he lay:
Christian children all must be
mild, obedient, good as he.

For he is our childhood's pattern,
day by day like us he grew;
he was little, weak and helpless,
tears and smiles like us he knew:
And he feeleth for our sadness,
and he shareth in our gladness.

And our eyes at last shall see him,
through his own redeeming love,
for that child so dear and gentle
is our Lord in heaven above;
and he leads his children on
to the place where he is gone.

Not in that poor lowly stable,
with the oxen standing by,
we shall see him; but in heaven,
set at God's right hand on high;
when like stars his children crowned
all in white shall wait around.

in royal David's city' was set to Henry Gauntlett's solemn tune 'Irby'. Recently she has been taken to task for some of her verses. A verse from 'All things bright and beautiful' about the 'rich man in his castle, the poor man at his gate' is routinely omitted. Even her familiar lines from 'Once in royal David's city', 'Christian children all must be mild, obedient, good as he', have been altered or removed from some recent hymn books. Perhaps their editors think that her words do not do justice to the example of acceptance and forgiveness set by Christ.

Mrs Alexander was writing in an age when childhood was unprivileged. Children were treated as small, inadequate adults.

Even middle-class children were expected to remain silent and pious in their nurseries. And for poor children there was the harsh, unfair world of slavery described so graphically by Charles Dickens. Mrs Alexander was writing to help children living through the realities of her time, and it was wise advice to the children of her day to keep a low profile.

In 1848, when *Hymns for Little Children* was being published, Europe was in a state of revolutionary and political turmoil. Death, too, was always close at hand and was less sanitized than it is today. In Victorian Britain, regular Sunday afternoon visits to family graves were thought to be character-forming for children. In an anonymous poem of the time, the village blacksmith, in church on Sunday with his sons, hears his daughter singing in the choir and is reminded of his wife:

...her mother's voice
singing in Paradise;
he needs must think of her once more,
as in her grave she lies;
and with his hard, rough hand he wipes
a tear from out his eyes.

In the great Christmas music festivals held annually for almost 70 years in the Crystal Palace in South London, choirs of as many as 2,000 women all dressed in white would sing Handel's great oratorios and choruses. If they also included Mrs Alexander's Christmas hymn, it must have seemed as though the prophecy of God's 'children crowned all in white' contained in the last two lines had come true.

Meanwhile, for *Songs of Praise* Christmas 2004 from King's College, Cambridge, all the BBC technicians are dressed in black so they cannot be seen among the Christmas congregation waiting to begin. In silence, the director of music, Stephen Cleobury, leads the 'mild, obedient, good' choir forward in their white surplices and red cassocks, creating an atmosphere that perfectly fits Mrs Alexander's original words. The choir stands motionless until, without evident signal, a small treble starts to sing.

Invisible cameras and microphones together record the moment that I first heard on the radio at home on Christmas Eve 60 years ago, as my mother stood on a chair and wrestled to balance holly on the picture rail, and my brother and I were being not so much mild and obedient as wild and excited. The sound from the radio arrested us all, and we became still and silent.

David Winter, a former Head of Religious Broadcasting at the BBC, has always insisted that the pictures are better on radio. Certainly, that original sound totally captured us all. But now, being there in King's College Chapel, it is a feast for the eyes, too, with the great, elegant organ case outlined against the intricately moulded ceiling of Henry VIII's Chapel.

I did not think that anything could match the real experience until I saw the TV broadcast a few days later. The camera director, David Kremer, had positioned the young treble so that you could see the triptych 'The Adoration of the Magi' over his shoulder, with the child lying in the manger. Here in one opening shot, combining light and deep shadow, is an image of childhood innocence and vulnerability in a dark world. As the young voice begins to sing, it is a moment of truth, of 'lambent' beauty, which none of us in the chapel had noticed.

As the TV cameras record us joining in with Mrs Alexander's deceptively simple hymn, we all begin to feel we are not merely retelling, but reliving the great story. It puts *Spiderman* and *Harry Potter* in the shade. Now that I have finally visited the set, I can begin to understand the movie.

See, amid the winter's snow
12

'It is how the nation goes to church,' said the BBC's Head of Religion and Ethics. Alan Bookbinder was describing TV broadcasts from St Paul's Cathedral. So many sad and happy occasions have taken place under the great dome in the last three centuries. We have been united in joy at royal weddings and jubilees, and when the Queen Mother celebrated her 100th birthday there in 2000; and we have grieved together at the funerals of our national heroes: Sir Winston Churchill in 1965 and, long before the age of TV, Admiral Lord Nelson in 1806. There have been few more moving *Songs of Praise* programmes than the one that took place on the evening of 31 August 1997, when stunned crowds filled the great nave of St Paul's to overflowing, to pray and sing hymns after the death of Diana, Princess of Wales.

I have a piece of flimsy, faded pink paper that I treasure, a reminder of yet another event in St Paul's. On it is printed a poem called 'Twenty Seventh February,

Sir John Goss by an unknown artist (1835)

1872', which celebrates the recovery of the then Prince of Wales from a very serious illness. Even Queen Victoria herself was persuaded to come out of her seclusion and attend the service of thanksgiving. It seems that my copy of the poem was one of many dropped out of the sky from a balloon floating over the cathedral, perhaps even onto the Queen's head:

Fear not, ye finder of this truant leaf,
Borne by the breeze to reach a hand unknown…

Thank heaven, now a nation's prayer prevails!
God bless the Queen! Long live the Prince of Wales!

27 February 1872 was also to be a red-letter day for another person, someone who played a big part in creating this service of thanksgiving for the Prince. John Goss had been organist of St Paul's for 34 years, and was knighted that same day by the Queen. His great moment of triumph was to come right at the end of his period of notice from the cathedral. He proudly announced that he was the only knight of the realm

See, amid the winter's snow,
born for us on earth below,
see, the tender Lamb appears
promised from eternal years!

Hail, thou ever-blessèd morn!
Hail, redemption's happy dawn!
Sing through all Jerusalem,
'Christ is born in Bethlehem!'

Lo! within a manger lies
he who built the starry skies,
he who, throned in height sublime,
sits amid the cherubim!

Say, ye holy shepherds, say,
what your joyful news today;
wherefore have ye left your sheep
on the lonely mountain steep?

'As we watched at dead of night,
lo, we saw a wondrous light:
angels singing, "Peace on earth"
told us of the Saviour's birth.'

Sacred Infant, all divine,
what a tender love was thine,
thus to come from highest bliss
down to such a world as this!

Teach, O teach us, holy Child,
by thy face so meek and mild,
teach us to resemble thee
in thy sweet humility.

living in the working-class suburb of Brixton. And it interested me to learn that just a few weeks earlier, he had written the tune for a new carol that is still one of the nation's favourites. He called his tune 'Humility'.

Sir John Goss was an appealing character who was always trying, usually without success, to please his colleagues – although his way of running his choir would not have been the model for the cathedral's present organist and regular judge of the *Songs of Praise* school choirs competition, Malcolm Archer. John Goss was a formidable musician with a naturally genial manner, who found himself surrounded by some unsavoury, very lazy and often absentee choristers. Several of them were ancient and could no longer sing, yet they still received a fee for being in the choir stalls. Sometimes the choir would even be singing one tune while he was playing another. One day when they were due to perform Handel's 'Hallelujah Chorus', the choir consisted of just two members: one tenor and one bass. 'Do your best!' Goss is said to have called down from the organ loft. In short, John Goss was a nice man and an appalling administrator.

In November 1871 matters had come to a head, and Goss no longer felt able to cope with the dean's constant criticism. He wrote his letter of resignation at the same time as he was composing his new Christmas carol tune, 'Humility', as a setting for Edward Caswall's words, 'See, amid the winter's snow'.

Goss may have chosen the words for the new carol to mark the arrival at the cathedral chapter of Henry Liddon, who was a great fan of Caswall's work in translating the hymns of the early church.

Edward Caswall himself had an interest in the Catholic and ritualistic wing of the church, and he had included the words in a poem that he wrote in 1858 called 'The Masque of Mary'.

Liddon, who was to have a profound influence on the services and preaching at St Paul's, would have been installed – probably at evensong – a month or two before Goss produced his tune. If Goss was trying one last time to turn over a new leaf, then we must be grateful that he did so with this spacious tune that continues to get everyone singing from the heart, as it did on *Songs of Praise* at Christmas 2004, from Ely Cathedral.

The carol begins by expressing wonder at the way God's promise is kept by the baby in the humble manger; the next two verses are a conversation with the shepherds on their journey; and then, with the shepherds safely arrived at Bethlehem, the carol ends as we all ask the holy child to teach us to follow him. The tune's name, 'Humility', perfectly sums up the message of the carol.

While this carol was being sung for *Songs of Praise* in Ely Cathedral, the director, David Kremer, trained the cameras on a beautiful nativity 'tableau vivant', designed by Carol Golder, which had been set up in the centre of the cathedral. Her Christmas scene had something of a Victorian garden arbour about it, and I could imagine Caswall and Goss thoroughly approving. However, as time went by, some 21st century additions did begin to creep in.

The 'characters' – shepherds, angels, wise men, Mary and Joseph – were all young children from one of the city's schools, dressed in traditional garb. They sat around the open-sided crib at the front of the nave under the gaze of their adoring parents. But recording *Songs of Praise* takes a very long time. They were all as good as gold (well, good-ish) for the first two hours; but by the time the cameras arrived to film them for 'See, amid the winter's snow', some were yawning, clearly ready for bed, and others were misbehaving, like the one armed with a shepherd's crook who had taken to biffing Mary on the head with it. Then there were the bottles of thoroughly modern juice that the director noticed had begun to appear in first-century Palestine...

The children were all stars, but it was a great relief to the congregation when, towards the end of a very long evening, after both carrot and stick had been proffered to the performers, they were finally allowed to break up the tableau and go home. Nevertheless, their moments on camera were very touching, and had helped us to understand what Edward Caswall's and John Goss's carol was all about. And perhaps, for some of the *Songs of Praise* audience, it was how they went to church that Christmas.

See him lying on a bed of straw
(Calypso carol)

10

Here is a carol that in four short lines takes us to the very heart of the incarnation:

O now carry me to Bethlehem
to see the Lord of love again:
just as poor as was the stable then,
the prince of glory when he came!

This is the best known of more than 300 songs, hymns and carols written by Michael Perry. Written to a dance rhythm – a reminder that the earliest carols were never intended just for singing – the Christmas story is told in the style of a West Indian calypso.

Michael Perry himself came from quite a different world from that of the warm, laid-back, song-filled Caribbean. I felt an extra sadness at his untimely, early death in 1996 because he was born in Beckenham in Kent in 1942, the same year and the same place as I was. Although we never met, I feel I have a little in common with him.

In the early 1950s, South London ended under the hill on which that wonder of the Victorian age, the Crystal Palace, had stood. The once-fashionable suburbs of Anerley and Penge marked the boundary between London and the county of Kent, and Beckenham's citizens took pride in being 'Kentish'. Penge had once had its own poet, Joseph Gwyer, but after being battered by flying enemy bombs at the end of the Second World War, it began to look as if its great days were over. Then new life began unexpectedly to pulsate through the streets of the tiny Victorian villas, bringing with it new sounds, bright clothes and a lively street life.

It began soon after the war in 1948 with the arrival of the liner *Empire Windrush*, the first of many ships to dock at Southampton bringing people to England from the islands of the Caribbean. Fifty years later, a moving *Songs of Praise* from Southwark Cathedral described the search for jobs and a new life in the heart of the Commonwealth that they belonged to. The country that they had learned about at school was where they were now needed.

For many of the people who came over, full of hope, and began work on the buses and in the hospitals of London, this was a hard time. England, and especially places like Penge where they first set up home, was inhospitably cold and dreary. The newcomers were treated with suspicion and hostility by the local people because of their colour and their different culture. Yet the music of the calypso soon crossed the boundary from Penge even into quiet and demure old Beckenham. If the young Michael Perry had stayed in his birthplace, he would have glimpsed this new world, as I did, on the buses and in the nearby street-markets. He would have heard their strange new music on the radio.

Even the BBC, in its slightly stuffy post-war ways, was broadcasting the Latin-American rhythms and the distinctive, story-telling style of the calypso on the *Light Programme*. It soon became fashionable, making stars of performers such as Cy Grant and Edmundo Ros. However, it was the newcomers on the streets of Britain who really put the experiences of their new life, both happy and sad, into song. Even the success or failure of the West Indian cricket team in the test match was celebrated with a calypso.

Jamaican immigrants welcomed by RAF officials from the Colonial Office after the ex-troopship *Empire Windrush* landed them at Tilbury

There was a bleaker side to this which reached our own quiet suburb. Uncomfortably close by, we could see people trying to live with dignity in run-down, squalid and overcrowded streets. Even my decent mother and father, who tried to help my brother and me feel safe and confident as we grew up in Beckenham, had difficulties with our new, lively and often very noisy neighbours. They disturbed our complacency and our consciences, just as the words of Michael Perry's carol are intended to.

I can never make up for the inaction of my younger days, but I am glad that, later in life, I was to direct one of the first *Songs of Praise* programmes to open a door to give a little space for the musical story of faith to be heard – told by the people who had grown

up so close by and yet in such different circumstances from my own. Perhaps Michael Perry discovered the words and rhythm of the 'Calypso Carol' with the same sense of gratitude. I don't know how much the West Indian community then or now have felt able to 'own' his calypso, but at least I can identify with his wish to try and enter their world.

Michael Perry was later to be a church leader, becoming Chairman of the Church Pastoral Aid Society and a member of the Church of England's governing body, the General Synod. For me, however, his enduring legacy will be this carol, which reminds me of the changing world in which I grew up.

'See him lying on a bed of straw' takes us to Bethlehem and shows us the birth 'on a bed of straw' in 'a draughty stable with an open door'. Sleepy shepherds are woken from their stupor and taken to see the Saviour of the world. Just as it took time for our own culture to understand that it was to become all the richer for the newcomers of the 1950s, so the song that the angels sang, the old Christmas story which tells us that 'Bethlehem's little baby' is the Saviour of us all, needs to be heard again and again.

A fifteenth-century nativity scene

See him lying on a bed of straw,
a draughty stable with an open door;
Mary cradling the babe she bore –
the prince of glory is his name.

O now carry me to Bethlehem
to see the Lord of love again:
just as poor as was the stable then,
the prince of glory when he came!

Star of silver, sweep across the skies,
show where Jesus in the manger lies;
shepherds, swiftly from your stupor rise
to see the saviour of the world!

Angels sing again the song you sang,
sing the glory of God's gracious plan;
sing that Bethlehem's little baby can
be the saviour of us all.

Mine are riches, from your poverty,
from your innocence, eternity;
mine forgiveness by your death for me,
child of sorrow for my joy.

Silent night

2

Looking out from a balcony in the old mountain-top village of Le Broc in the South of France, it seemed as though the whole Alpine region of Europe was visible below us, spread out along a wide river running through an enormous valley dotted with countless villages. One of the rewards of climbing a high mountain, or even a steep hill, is looking back down on the place you've come from. The busy, noisy world where the climb began appears to be silent and still. The ordinary town, spread out in miniature far below, now looks beautiful. Stone buildings on the valley floor look frail and vulnerable seen against a wider, more powerful, natural landscape.

The story of 'Silent night' began with just such an experience for the man who wrote the original German words, 'Stille Nacht', in 1818. Josef Mohr was a Roman Catholic priest in the Austrian village of Oberndorf. As he had only recently arrived in the village, he was invited to meet his new congregation by a neighbour, who arranged a meal and the performance of a nativity play at his home. Father Josef was so moved both by the hospitality and the play that before going home he climbed up the hillside in the dark to look back at the twinkling lights of the village newly in his care that Christmas time. As he looked

down, thinking all the while of the play performed at the fireside, the words, which have made such an impact on so many people and which are now familiar to us all, began to come to him:

Stille Nacht, heilege Nacht!
Alles schlaft, einsam wacht…

'Silent night, holy night! All is calm, all is bright…' is how the English translation, which most of us have known since childhood, begins; and these were the words sung in the 2004 Christmas *Songs of Praise* from the Royal Albert Hall by Hayley Westenra and Aled Jones. But if you look this Christmas hymn up in any hymn book, you may well find something else. The title may be 'Still the night', and there are other variations as different translators have tried to capture the essence of the original. 'All is calm, all is bright' becomes 'Sleeps the world; hid from sight' in the BBC *Songs of Praise* book, and 'Heaven is near, earth is bright' in the *New English Hymnal*. As well as all the various English versions, Josef Mohr's words have now been translated into more than a hundred different languages.

Perhaps it is the story of the tune as much as the background to the words that has so caught the universal imagination. Father Josef completed his hymn before he went to sleep that night, and the next morning, which was Christmas Eve, he showed it to his church organist, Franz Gruber. According to the story, the church organ had broken down; but Herr Gruber composed a tune for the hymn that day, to be played on the guitar. At their Christmas Eve mass that night, the hymn – set for two voices and

chorus just like Aled and Hayley's version for *Songs of Praise* – had its first performance.

Gruber's solution to the lack of an organ must have seemed like a small miracle for the congregation that night, just as it did a few years ago at our local Roman Catholic church in a Kentish village when the organ collapsed seconds before a wedding, and one of the guests saved the day by producing a guitar. *Songs of Praise* has not escaped these kinds of emergencies either, and I still remember, back in the 1970s, the barely concealed terror and fervent prayer with which I greeted choirs and congregation to a recording when there was a power cut. I know how Father Josef must have felt at Christmas in 1818.

'Silent night' has been sung all around the world, but never did it create a stranger alliance than when, nearly a hundred years after its composition, fighting men from two nations at war suspended hostilities to sing the words together. No one is left alive to describe what really led to the truce and the legendary game of football in no-man's land on the Western Front at Christmas in 1914; but we can be fairly certain that it was the German soldiers who would have begun the singing on Christmas Eve.

In Germany Christmas Eve was, and still is, the day when Christmas is celebrated. It is the night for singing 'O Tannenbaum' ('O Christmas tree'), and celebrating the decorating of the tree, with its message of peace: 'You bear a joyful message: That faith and hope shall ever bloom to bring us light in winter's gloom.' And, of course, to sing 'Stille Nacht'.

My wife Liz's grandfather came from

Germany as a child in the 1890s, to live in the North of England, where he continued for the rest of his life to celebrate Christmas in the German way – on Christmas Eve. He would bring into the house the *Tannenbaum*, which he always decorated himself behind closed doors. Towards midnight, when all was ready, he would blow a horn, the signal for his children – Liz's father and his brothers – to charge excitedly down the stairs to see the richly decorated, candle-lit tree, with its nativity scene below, surrounded by presents. Then, each one the possessor of a fine baritone or bass voice, they would sing carols in German – the only words in the language that they were ever taught, but which they were to remember all their lives.

To celebrate Liz's father's 80th birthday

in 1993, we made a surprise video of family memories, which includes a now treasured recording of the Christmas hymn sung in German by his last remaining brother. We went to Liz's uncle Fred's house in Manchester, where, accompanied by his son John on the guitar, Fred sang 'Stille Nacht' and then gestured to us all, including me, the shaking cameraman, to join him in singing it in English.

A *Songs of Praise* viewer called John, when voting for 'Silent night', wrote in describing another moment of reconciliation between the one-time enemies. Growing up in Wales after the Second World War, he lived close to a camp housing 2,000 German prisoners-of-war. By Christmas 1946 he had befriended one officer in particular, who was working in the fields nearby. To his astonishment, the officer asked him to come into the camp to share the POWs' Christmas

Silent night, holy night!
All is calm all is bright
'round yon virgin mother and child,
holy infant so tender and mild.
Sleep in heavenly peace,
sleep in heavenly peace.

Silent night, holy night!
Shepherds quake at the sight.
Glories stream from heaven afar,
heav'nly hosts sing Alleluia;
Christ the Saviour is born;
Christ the Saviour is born.

Silent night, holy night!
Son of God, love's pure light.
Radiant beams from thy holy face,
with the dawn of redeeming grace,
Jesus, Lord, at thy birth;
Jesus, Lord, at thy birth.

dinner. They first had to lend him a prison uniform so that he could get past the British camp guards! Once safely inside, John was asked to join their carol service, in which the singing was accompanied by an organ the prisoners had made themselves. 'When we came to sing "Silent night, holy night"' writes John 'all the men rose to sing this one – and how they sang it... their feelings and emotions were infectious; and I thought,

How did we become such bitter enemies? It seemed so insane... The words of Jesus Christ impressed themselves on my soul... "If your enemy is hungry, feed him".'

In 1997, almost 180 years after the Christmas Eve when 'Silent night' was first sung, three more verses of Father Josef's hymn were discovered. One verse surely reveals what the young priest hoped we would all understand:

Silent night, holy night!
God pours down, full of might,
Father's love on the whole human race,
yet as brother is glad to embrace
Jesus, born for us all!
Jesus, born for us all!

Can any late-night stroll up a mountain-side ever have been more productive?

The holly and the ivy
14

On Christmas Day our old stable in Midlothian is as bare as the nearby turkey farm. I once filmed such a farm for *Songs of Praise* and, having made a lot of eye contact with birds whose days are so numbered in December, I am glad to say that at home we no longer eat turkey for Christmas. The activity in our stable in the run-up to Christmas is altogether more gentle in its nature. Our neighbour, Billy, makes more than a hundred wreaths in there. Originally the manufacture took place in a small greenhouse, but due to high demand Billy has had to expand into our large, stone stable. He works in the dim, almost holy light of one small window, turning the piles of moss, ivy and berried holly he has gathered from the woods into traditional Christmas wreaths.

The carol that brings holly and ivy together is a reminder of the pagan festival of Yule, when bringing evergreens into the house in the darkest season of the year was thought to ward off evil spirits. Even the song

85

The holly and the ivy,
when they are both full grown,
of all the trees that are in the wood,
the holly bears the crown.

The rising of the sun
and the running of the deer,
the playing of the merry organ,
sweet singing in the choir.

The holly bears a blossom
as white as the lily flower,
and Mary bore sweet Jesus Christ
to be our sweet Saviour.

The holly bears a berry
as red as any blood,
and Mary bore sweet Jesus Christ
to do poor sinners good.

The holly bears a prickle
as sharp as any thorn,
and Mary bore sweet Jesus Christ
on Christmas Day in the morn.

The holly bears a bark
as bitter as any gall,
and Mary bore sweet Jesus Christ
for to redeem us all.

itself is pre-Christian and was probably originally a circle dance – the holly symbolising the masculine and the ivy the feminine – performed by the men and women carrying them.

The song survived even the grim strictness of Oliver Cromwell's Puritans, who banned all carol singing, and was among the ancient folk tunes collected by young musicians Cecil Sharp and Ralph Vaughan Williams a century ago. Cecil Sharp noted it down from an old lady living in the Cotswold village of Chipping Campden, and more verses were later discovered by Ralph Vaughan Williams.

To have holly bushes in the garden that actually produce berries is a real treat for me. In our childhood garden we had a huge holly tree, armed to the teeth with prickles but entirely devoid of berries. (I now know, having married a gardener, that you need two holly trees if you want berries.) I can remember the smell and the feel of that old

tree even now, because you could squeeze through a gap in its branches and be hidden safe and dry behind its dense greenery, even during a snowstorm.

These evergreens, which bear prickles, berries and fruit even when the rest of nature seems dead, showed our ancestors the triumph of life over death. It was a first recognition, drawn from nature in the depth of winter, of the hope of resurrection, which is why the old song transforms so well into a Christmas carol.

In our stable on Christmas Eve, the last few holly wreaths are adorned with white lilies before being taken round the village. A few will be placed on people's front doors, but many more will be laid on the graves of loved ones in the quiet churchyard, while inside the church we celebrate once more with 'the playing of the merry organ, sweet singing in the choir'.

While shepherds watched
17

For many, one of the BBC TV highlights of 2004 was the return of *One Man and his Dog*, the programme in which shepherds and their dogs compete with other contestants to corral a small bunch of sometimes very muddled sheep into a pen. One secret of the programme's appeal, of course, is the working sheepdog. It is the dog that we want to watch, as it responds obediently to a strange mixture of whistles and shouts from the shepherd standing at a distance. It is a traditional country pursuit, and a heart-warming relationship for townees – who normally see sheep only as part of the scenery as they speed through – to watch. What is it about this picture of the shepherd, his dog and his sheep that is so appealing?

The real life of a shepherd, as *Songs of Praise* has often shown, is much harder than it looks, and it can often be a very lonely existence being out in all weathers on the moors and hills. It is rare to see more than one shepherd, and for a short but terrible time a few years ago in the border country of England and Scotland that I drive through, it was even rare to see more than one, if any, sheep. Every passing traveller must thank God that the foot and mouth epidemic has passed almost as much as the farmers and shepherds whose lives

were so devastated by it. We need to see sheep, and the sheep need a shepherd.

Filming sheep for *Songs of Praise* can be a frustrating experience for a TV director, especially one who has in mind the traditional Christmas card picture of a flock surging peacefully across a sunny, snowy

Adoration of the Shepherds by Dosso Dossi and Battista Dossi (c. 1535–1536)

87

landscape while a shepherd and his dog survey the scene with a calm smile. Twenty-five years ago I was once again trying it myself in the Scottish borders, and I still often drive past the field where the first flock I tried filming that day disappeared into the most distant corner as soon as the camera was set up. The shepherd did his best, but his sheepdogs seemed to be on strike and we eventually gave up.

At our next location, a redoubtable if rather elderly peer of the realm revealed that she had sheep she was certain would be happy to be filmed. Almost before the camera was out of the car, this kindly lady, dressed in stout shoes and tweeds and without the aid of a dog, was rushing towards her herd calling 'Sheep! Sheep! Sheep!' The sheep scattered.

The baroness was not to be defeated, and she went to where they had gathered at the farthest end of her field and began driving them towards us, intending that we should get a close-up of approaching sheep. I did not have the heart to use the only shots I did achieve, as in all of them the good baroness was quite clearly visible in the background, galloping cheerfully through the field behind the panicking sheep, waving her arms in a thoroughly Pythonesque style while the accelerating flock ran helter-skelter towards us, before swerving off and scattering in all directions.

'While shepherds watched their flocks by night' takes us into a scene in rural first-century Palestine, a typical picture that we might have witnessed at any time in the 2,000 years since: shepherds out in the fields, looking after their flocks. In the middle of an ordinary night something extraordinary breaks into their routine, and the hymn is really a paraphrase of the events described in chapter 2 of Luke's Gospel.

The man who turned the Bible story into a hymn in 1699 was Nahum Tate, an Irishman who was poet laureate for William and Mary. Scots reformers of the time translated the opening verse as 'While

humble shepherds watched their flocks'. Tate was one of a group of people who, responding to the Reformation that had swept through Europe, provided the first metrical psalms and hymns that could be sung congregationally. Everything they wrote was drawn from the Bible, and was intended to put into practice a verse from the letter of James:

Is anyone among you suffering? Let him pray. Is anyone cheerful? Let him sing praise.
JAMES 5:13

The six verses of 'While shepherds watched' are a simple retelling of the gospel story about which we can all agree. Coming to a consensus on the tune, however, is a different matter. 'Winchester Old', which many call the 'old' tune, was originally

published in 1592 for the metrical version of Psalm 84, 'How lovely is thy dwelling place, O Lord of hosts, to me!', and was then used by Nahum Tate for his carol. All fans of the late Dame Thora Hird, however, will remember that for her the only 'right' tune was Thomas Jarman's 'Lyngham', which she remembered hearing on Christmas mornings in Morecambe. It is a tune most of us would associate with Charles Wesley's 'O for a thousand tongues to sing', but the BBC *Songs of Praise* hymn book honours Dame Thora by tactfully printing it as the second tune to 'While shepherds watched'.

There is another tune, which I remember learning at school to the words of 'On Ilkley Moor ba' t'at'. They use this tune, naturally enough, in Yorkshire, where they have a Christmas tradition of singing Christmas carols in the inns and pubs.

For the 2004 Christmas *Songs of Praise* from Ely Cathedral, the organist Paul Trepte broke away from the familiar and combined the traditional words with a new refrain. He then set the whole thing to a tune that I had only ever previously heard played by a Salvation Army band. The effect on the nation's favourite carol poll was a dramatic rise in votes for 'While shepherds watched', almost certainly influenced by the new arrangement and the tune they sang that night, 'Sweet chiming Christmas bells'.

All anyone could tell me about the tune was that it originated from 'Spoforth's Collection'. And so began my long and almost demented search using the so-called 'wonders' of the worldwide web. Late into the night I sat in front of the computer. Who is – or was – Spoforth and his collection? The web, as it does, helpfully put me in touch with garages in the mid-west of

While shepherds watched their flocks
   by night,
all seated on the ground,
the angel of the Lord came down,
and glory shone around.

'Fear not,' said he (for mighty dread
had seized their troubled mind),
'glad tidings of great joy I bring
to you and all mankind.

'To you in David's town this day
is born of David's line
a Saviour, who is Christ the Lord;
and this shall be the sign:

'The heavenly Babe you there shall find
to human view displayed,
all meanly wrapped in swathing-bands,
and in a manger laid.'

Thus spake the seraph; and forthwith
appeared a shining throng
of angels, praising God, who thus
addressed their joyful song:

'All glory be to God on high,
and to the world be peace!
Goodwill henceforth from heaven
   to earth
begin and never cease!'

America, obscure parish records in Cumbria and a list of relatives attending a wedding in Australia; but no collector or composer of hymn tunes.

Then there were the words of the refrain. Where had they come from?

Those chiming Christmas bells,
sweet chiming Christmas bells.
They cheer us on our heavenly way
those chiming bells.

Friends vaguely remembered singing the words in gospel halls and Baptist chapels years ago, but no one knew or could remember the name of the author. Back to the computer, which produced thousands of references to chiming bells, and especially the American custom of using chimes at church services. I found myself scanning through countless Canadian and American church newsletters. (On the way, I incidentally discovered how seriously detrimental the effect of a 'white' Christmas can be on remote communities...)

The answer I needed was closer to home, and, as ever, it was the Salvation Army who supplied it. Just when I was about to give up, they pointed me to Brigadier Miriam Richards. Brigadier Richards, who died not long ago, used to help produce the Army's magazine *The War Cry*. It was her words that Paul Trepte used as a refrain at the end of each verse of Nahum Tate's great seventeenth-century paraphrase of Luke's account of the birth of Jesus. And, whatever purists may feel, the refrain does somehow involve each one of us more deeply in the story as it unfolds.

For now, I have given up on the elusive Spoforth. His jolly tune is an old favourite for brass band enthusiasts, and the instrumentalists in Ely Cathedral were clearly having as much fun as the singers. Paul Trepte believes that it comes from Yorkshire, and perhaps it was once sung in nineteenth-century chapels and churches where motley bands of musicians used to play the music for worship before the days of the church organ. It is a mystery I leave for any curious reader of this book to solve.

Epilogue

At Christmas, more than ever, TV plays a big part in most of our lives. Some people think that watching TV is a private, even a lonely, occupation; but the annual broadcast by the Queen and episodes of high drama from the popular soap operas draw millions of viewers every Christmas. Viewing becomes a shared experience, discussed in telephone conversations and e-mails, down at the pub with friends or back

at work with colleagues in the new year. It is not so very different from the story-sharing of Mr Pickwick and his friends in Charles Dickens's world, a century and a half ago.

Tempted by the thought of memories from Christmases past, I watched a special programme of 100 clips of 'The nation's all-time favourite Christmas moments', and was glad to see that *Carols from King's College, Cambridge* was included in the final

countdown. As in a Dickens's book, the harsh realities of life were not excluded. The most unsettling clip, one that too often still haunts our news, was of starving and dying babies, innocents caught up in war and famine. Just before Christmas 1984, an array of famous pop stars had responded to this image by coming together to try to change the world. After all the news reports of a famine of biblical proportions in Ethiopia, the singers Bob Geldof and Midge Ure made an appeal that led in 1985 to *Live Aid*, a global TV broadcast uniting famous rock stars and millions of their fans in fundraising on an unprecedented scale. The song they all recorded begins on a note of irony:

It's Christmas time,
there's no need to be afraid.

And concludes with the chorus:

Feed the world.
Let them know it's Christmas time.

It led to sales of three and a half million records, raising eight million pounds of aid. Twenty years later, after the song was re-recorded and re-released by Band Aid 20, a group of present-day pop artists, Bob Geldof said of the original, 'We were just a couple of geezers doing their bit... Maybe the people who bought it are now in positions of power.'

Almost eighty years ago, two other 'geezers', Philip Heseltine, a composer, and his friend Bruce Blunt, had both fallen on hard times. They were broke. So they entered a competition for new carols being run by the *Daily Telegraph*. According to them, after a night of drinking and revelry they sat down together and wrote the words and music for a beautiful carol which was to win first prize. Unfortunately, it seems that after the celebration that followed all the prize money was gone; and by 1930 the composer, better known by his pseudonym, Peter Warlock, had died tragically young.

But what remains is the haunting 'Bethlehem down', a carol that choirs will always want to sing and we to listen to. Among all our familiar, cheerful carols, 'Bethlehem down' provides an intensely thoughtful and spiritual contrast. The dark shadow of the cross hangs over this carol, but love, peace and humanity also have their gentle moment:

Here he has peace and a short while for
*   dreaming,*
close huddled oxen to keep him from cold,
Mary for love and for lullaby music,
songs of a shepherd by Bethlehem fold.

These days the new kids on the block are Keith Getty and Stuart Townend, who collaborate to write hymns and songs based on scripture. They are working on a project called 'Creed', hymns and songs based on the Apostles' Creed, just as Mrs Alexander was doing in her *Songs for Little Children*.

Stuart says, 'Keith and I both share a passion to see churches singing songs full of truth, compositions that not only express our love and devotion to God, but also declare the wonderful truths of the faith – truths that form the foundations of our lives.'

They hope their new carol, 'Joy has dawned upon the world', will provide something for everyone. Here is the final verse, pointing to what is to come for the baby born in the stable:

Son of Adam, Son of heaven,
Given as a ransom,
Reconciling God and man,
Christ our mighty Champion!
What a Saviour, what a Friend,
What a glorious mystery:
Once a babe in Bethlehem,
Now the Lord of history

As I began the search for the nation's favourite carol, I was startled when a friend in our village without any hesitation nominated as his choice Isaac Watts's 'When I survey the wondrous cross'. 'But that's a Good Friday hymn,' I said. Commenting on my surprise, the preacher and broadcaster Colin Morris provides a final thought: 'But it is also good theology at Christmas time.'

While we've seen how many of the most popular carols were written in the nineteenth century, it would be wrong to conclude that carols belong only to a sentimental, Victorian Christmas card past. I hope I have been able to show how much even the very oldest of these carols still has the power to shake us up and wake us up to God's presence in the world in our own troubled times. The new story has only just begun.

The Top Twenty

1. In the bleak mid-winter

2. Silent night

3. Hark! the herald-angels sing

4. O holy night

5. O come all ye faithful

6. It came upon the midnight clear

7. O little town of Bethlehem

8. Once in royal David's city

9. Away in a manger

10. See him lying on a bed of straw (*Calypso carol*)

11. Long time ago in Bethlehem (*Mary's boy child*)

12. See, amid the winter's snow

13. On Christmas night all Christians sing (*Sussex carol*)

14. The holly and the ivy

15. Christians, awake

16. God rest you merry, gentlemen

17. While shepherds watched

18. Joy to the world

19. In dulci jubilo

20. Good King Wenceslas

Text Acknowledgments

p. 35: 'In dulci jubilo' taken from *The Popular Carol Book*, edited by Richard J. Coleman, Geoffrey Court and Rosalind Russell. Reprinted by permission of The Continuum International Publishing Group.

p. 51 'Mary's boy child': Words and Music by Jester Hairston © Copyright 1956, 1957 by Schumann Music Corp. Copyright Renewed. World Rights Controlled by Bourne Co. All Rights Reserved. International Copyright Secured. Printed with permission from Bourne Music Ltd.

p. 67: 'A Bidding Prayer' taken from *Daily Prayer* compiled by Eric Milner-White, copyright © 1941 Oxford University Press.

p. 79: 'See him lying on a bed of straw': words: Michael Perry © Mrs B Perry / Jubilate Hymns, 4 Thorne Park Road, Torquay TQ2 6RX, www.jubilate.co.uk. Used by permission.

p. 84: Additional verse for 'Silent Night' taken from *The Popular Carol Book*, edited by Richard J. Coleman, Geoffrey Court and Rosalind Russell. Reprinted by permission of The Continuum International Publishing Group.

p. 89 Scripture quotation taken from the Revised Standard Version published by HarperCollins Publishers, copyright © 1989 by the Division of Christian Education of the National Council of the Churches of Christ in the USA, and are used by permission. All rights reserved.

pp. 93 'Do They Know It's Christmas': Words and Music by Bob Geldof and Midge Ure © 1985 Chappell Music Ltd, London W6 8BS. Lyrics reproduced by permission of IMP Ltd. All Rights Reserved.

p. 94: Extract from 'Joy has dawned upon the World' by Keith Getty and Stuart Townend, copyright © 2004 Thankyou Music. Administered by worshiptogether.com songs excluding UK and Europe, administered by Kingsway Music. tym@kingsway.co.uk. Used by permission.

Picture Acknowledgments

All images © Andrew Barr, except where noted below.

p. 4 copyright © Andy Rous

p. 24 copyright © Dover Publications

pp.30–31 copyright © Lion Hudson

pp. 50–51 copyright © Steve Murray / Alamy

p. 57 copyright © nagelestock.com / Alamy

p. 66 copyright © Howard Taylor / Alamy

pp. 82–83 copyright © Agence Images / Alamy

p. 84 copyright © allOver photography / Alamy

p. 85 copyright © David Boag / Alamy

pp. 88–89 copyright © mediacolor's / Alamy

Picture research on the following pages courtesy of Zooid Pictures Limited: pp 11 Summerfield Press/Corbis UK Ltd., 16 Ronald Grant Archive, 17 National Portrait Gallery, 21 Sandro Vannini/Corbis UK Ltd., 22 Ronald Grant Archive, 25 Mary Evans Picture Library, 26 Mary Evans Picture Library, 29 Mary Evans Picture Library, 34 David Lees/Corbis UK Ltd., 38 Sotheby's/AKG – Images, 39 AKG – Images, 43 Reuters/Corbis UK Ltd., 46 Mary Evans Picture Library, 49 Granger Collection, 50 Bettmann/Corbis UK Ltd., 52 National Portrait Gallery, 54 Francis G. Mayer/Corbis UK Ltd., 58 PA/Empics, 61 Rex Features, 62 Reuters/Corbis UK Ltd., 64 Bettmann/Corbis UK Ltd., 65 Mary Evans Picture Library, 69 Mary Evans Picture Library, 72 National Portrait Gallery, 77 PA/Empics, 78 Philadelphia Museum of Art/Corbis UK Ltd., 87 Arte & Immagini srl/Corbis UK Ltd., 92–93 Rex Features